American Red Cross

Together, we can save a life

USA
UNITED STATES OLYMPIC COMMITTEE
36 USC 380

SPORT SAFETY TRAINING

INJURY PREVENTION AND CARE

COURSE WORKBOOK

StayWell

StayWell

SPORT SAFETY TRAINING WORKBOOK

This participant's workbook is an integral part of the American Red Cross Sport Safety Training course. By itself, it does not constitute complete and comprehensive training for first aid. Please contact your Red Cross chapter or station for further information on this course.

The emergency care procedures outlined in this book reflect the standard of knowledge and accepted emergency practices in the United States at the time this book was published. It is the reader's responsibility to stay informed of changes in the emergency care procedures. By itself, this book does not constitute complete and comprehensive training.

Printed in the United States of America

Composition by Graphic World, Inc.
Printing/Binding by Banta

Photo Credit: Cover Images by Getty Images. Sasha Andrews kicks the ball away from Mia Hamm (Photo by Jeff Gross/Getty Images). Olympics Swimming (Photo by Simon Bruty/Getty Images). Special Olympics World Games (Photo by Rick stewart/Allsport).

StayWell
780 Township Line Rd.
Yardley, PA 19067-4200

ISBN 1-58480-223-5

04 05 06 07 08/ 9 8 7 6 5 4 3 2 1

ACKNOWLEDGMENTS

The original version of this manual was developed through a combined effort of the American Red Cross and the United States Olympic Committee. Without the commitment to excellence of employees and volunteers of both organizations, this manual could not have been created.

Revision Team
The American Red Cross Sport Safety Training course and supporting materials were developed through the dedication of both employees and volunteers. Their commitment to excellence made this course possible.

The following individuals contributed to the development and review of this course and supporting materials.

The American Red Cross, Sport Safety Training project team included:

Project Team

John Beales
Manager
Preparedness—Products Management & Program Administration
American Red Cross National Headquarters
Falls Church, Virginia

Betty J. Butler
Administrative Support
Preparedness—Research and Product Development
Falls Church, Virginia

Ted T. Crites, CHES
Project Manager
Preparedness—Technical Development, Research and Product Development
American Red Cross National Headquarters
Falls Church, Virginia

Marc Madden
Sr. Associate
Preparedness—Technical Development, Research and Product Development
American Red Cross National Headquarters
Falls Church, VA

Kyle Majchrzak
Associate
Preparedness—Products Management
American Red Cross National Headquarters
Falls Church, Virginia

Adreania McMillian
Associate
Preparedness—Technical Development, Research and Product Development
American Red Cross National Headquarters
Falls Church, Virginia

Heather Overstreet
Sr. Associate
Communications and Marketing
American Red Cross National Headquarters
Washington, DC

Rick Sleutaris
Sr. Associate
Preparedness—Operations
American Red Cross National Headquarters
Falls Church, Virginia

John Thompson
Associate
Preparedness—Products Management
Falls Church, Virginia

Jane Wiehe, RN
American Red Cross
Cincinnati Area Chapter
Cincinnati, Ohio

External/Chapter Reviewers

Sherri Lynn Almeida
Advisory Council on First Aid and Safety
Team Health Southwest
Bellaire, Texas

Sandra Rae Badger
Cross Country/Track Coach
Intercollegiate Athletics
University of Colorado at Colorado Springs
Colorado Springs, Colorado

Donna Cunningham
Volunteer
Boy Scouts of America Venturing Division
Amarillo, Texas

Larry Cunningham
Volunteer
Boy Scouts of America Venturing Division
Amarillo, Texas

T. Douglas Coyle, MSHS, CHES
American Red Cross
Dallas Area Chapter
Dallas, Texas

Janice DeAngelis
Director, Health & Safety
American Red Cross
Lorain County Chapter
Elyria, Ohio.

Larry Decker
Education Specialist
American Red Cross
Pikes Peak Chapter
Colorado Springs, Colorado

Jennifer B. Hair
American Red Cross
Dallas Area Chapter
Specialist, Emergency Preparedness
Dallas, Texas

John Kaufmann
Supervisory Training Specialist
Naval Aviation Schools Command, Survival Department
Pensacola Naval Air Station, Florida

Allen Kipp
Director of Health and Safety
American Red Cross
Birmingham Area Chapter
Birmingham, Alabama

Paul R. Levins
PTI Coordinator
Naval Aviation Schools Command, Survival Department
Pensacola Naval Air Station, Florida

James C. O'Leary MS, ATC/L
Certified Athletic Trainer
Cleveland Clinic Sports Health
Lorain, Ohio

Sanford (Sandy) Miller, ATC, LAT
Head Athletic Trainer
Stephen F. Austin State University
SFA Station
Nacogodoches, Texas

Cathy Sellers
Manager, Coaching
United States Olympic Committee
Colorado Springs, Colorado

M. Kathryn Scott
Advisory Council on First Aid and Safety
Department of Physical Education
University of California
Berkeley, California

Murray Stephens
USA Swimming
Meadowbrook Aquatic Center
Baltimore, Maryland

Cindy Tow, RN
American Red Cross
Birmingham Area Chapter
Birmingham, AL

Dave Thomas
USA Swimming
Sport Development Consultant
Colorado Springs, Colorado
Southern Zone

StayWell

The StayWell editorial and production team included:

Nancy Monahan
Senior Vice President

Bill Winneberger
Senior Director of Manufacturing

Donna Balado
Director of Editorial

Paula Batt
Director of Sales

Reed Klanderud
Director of Marketing

Amanda Land
Marketing Manager

Jo Ann Emenecker
Editorial Project Manager

Laura O'Leary
Senior Production Manager

Louise Quinn
Publications Coordinator

Acknowledgments
In addition to the United States Olympic Committee, the following organizations provided expert review of the materials and support for the American Red Cross Sport Safety Training Program:

VENTURING®·BSA

National Athletic Trainers' Association

NAVAL AVIATION SCHOOLS COMMAND

USA SWIMMING®

Front Matter Note:

Sports injury research continues to evolve and to provide more detailed information on the exact causes and most beneficial emergency care of injury. It is recommended that Sport Safety Training participants stay current in ongoing research on the causes, prevention and care of sports injury.

In this workbook, the term "athlete" is used generically and may refer to any individual including coaches, officials, parents, etc.

CONTENTS

1
LESSON

INTRODUCTION—BEFORE PROVIDING CARE

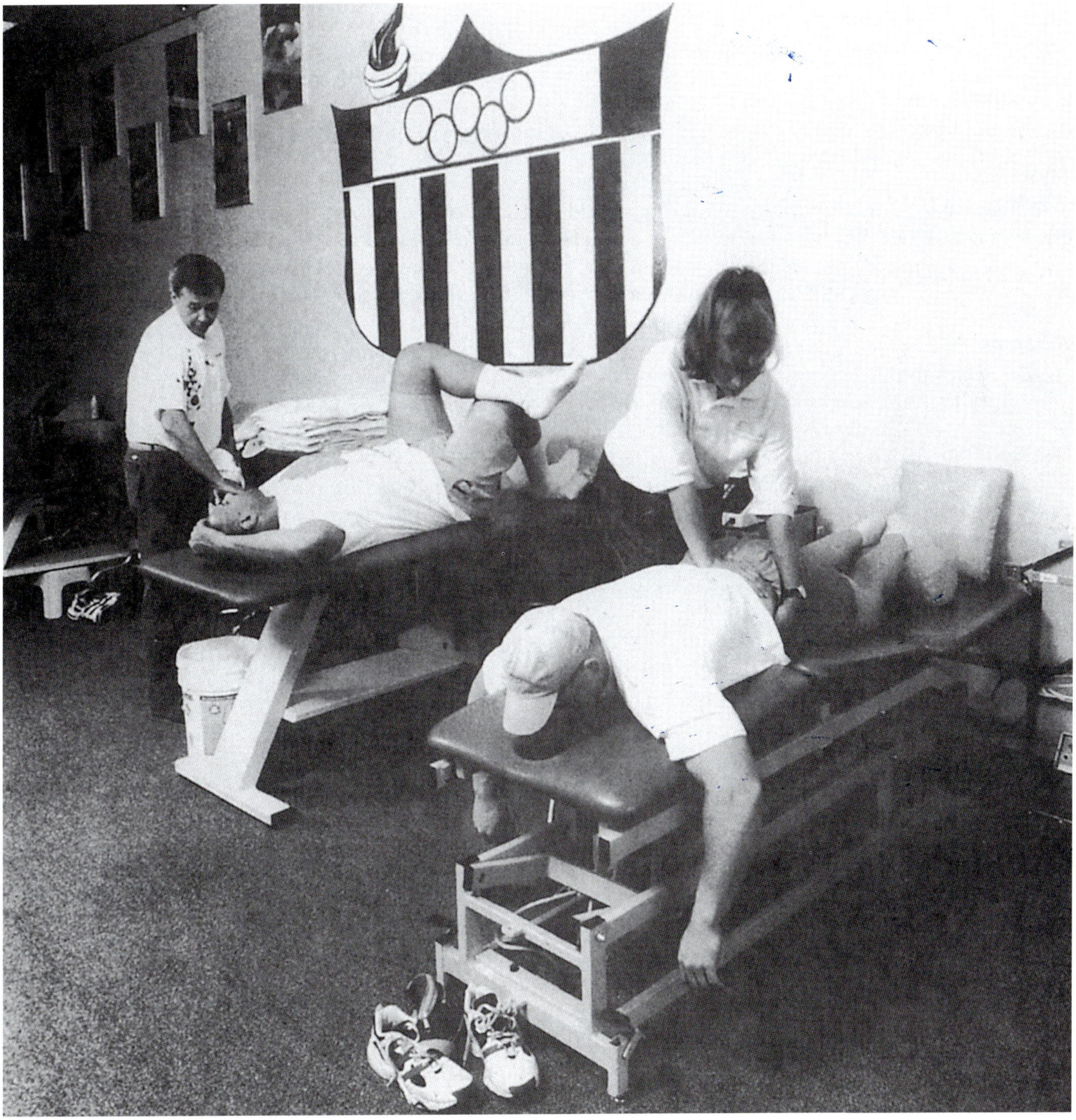

1
LESSON

INTRODUCTION—BEFORE PROVIDING CARE

COURSE INTRODUCTION

Health Precautions and Guidelines During Training

The American Red Cross has trained millions of people in first aid and CPR (cardiopulmonary resuscitation) using manikins as training aids. According to the Centers for Disease Control (CDC), there has never been a documented case of any disease caused by bacteria, a fungus or a virus transmitted through the use of training aids such as manikins used for CPR.

The Red Cross follows widely accepted guidelines for cleaning and decontaminating training manikins. **If these guidelines are adhered to, the risk of any kind of disease transmission during training is extremely low.**

To help minimize the risk of disease transmission, you should follow some basic health precautions and guidelines while participating in training. You should take precautions if you have a condition that would increase your risk or other participants' risk of exposure to infections. Request a separate training manikin if you:

- Have an acute condition, such as a cold, a sore throat, cuts or sores on the hands or around your mouth.
- Know you are seropositive (have had a positive blood test) for hepatitis B surface antigen (HBsAg), indicating that you are currently infected with the hepatitis B virus*.
- Know you have a chronic infection indicated by long-term seropositivity (long-term positive blood tests) for the hepatitis B surface antigen (HBsAg)* or a positive blood test for anti-human immunodeficiency virus (HIV); that is, a positive test for antibodies to HIV, the virus that causes many severe infections including acquired immunodeficiency syndrome (AIDS).
- Have had a positive blood test for hepatitis C (HCV).
- Have a type of condition that makes you unusually likely to get an infection.

To obtain information about testing for individual health status, go to: www.cdc.gov/ncidod/diseases/hepatitis/c/faq.htm

*A person with hepatitis B infection will test positive for the hepatitis B surface antigen (HBsAg). Most persons infected with hepatitis B will get better within a period of time. However, some hepatitis B infections will become chronic and will linger for much longer. These persons will continue to test positive for HBsAg. Their decision to participate in CPR training should be guided by their physician.

After a person has had an acute hepatitis B infection, he or she will no longer test positive for the surface antigen but will test positive for the hepatitis B antibody (anti-HBs). Persons who have been vaccinated for hepatitis B will also test positive for the hepatitis antibody. A positive test for the hepatitis B antibody (anti-HBs) should not be confused with a positive test for the hepatitis B surface antigen (HBsAG).

If you decide you should have your own manikin, ask your instructor if he or she can provide one for you to use. You will **not** be asked to explain why in your request. The manikin will not be used by anyone else until it has been cleaned according to the recommended end-of-class decontamination procedures. Because the number of manikins available for class use is limited, the more advance notice you give, the more likely it is that you can be provided a separate manikin.

Guidelines

In addition to taking the precautions regarding manikins, you can further protect yourself and other participants from infection by following these guidelines:

- Wash your hands thoroughly before participating in class activities.
- Do not eat, drink, use tobacco products or chew gum during class when manikins are used.
- Clean the manikin properly before use.
  - For some manikins, this means vigorously wiping the manikin's face and the inside of its mouth with a clean gauze pad soaked with either a fresh solution of liquid chlorine bleach and water (¼ c sodium hypochlorite per gallon of tap water) or rubbing alcohol. The surfaces should remain wet for at least 30 seconds before they are wiped dry with a second piece of clean, absorbent material.

- For other manikins, it means changing the manikin's face. Your instructor will provide you with instructions for cleaning the type of manikin used in your class.

- Follow the guidelines provided by your instructor when practicing skills such as clearing a blocked airway with your finger.

Physical Stress and Injury

Successful course completion requires full participation in classroom and skill sessions, as well as successful performance in skill and knowledge evaluations. Due to the nature of the skills in this course, you will be participating in strenuous activities, such as performing CPR on the floor. If you have a medical condition or disability that will prevent you from taking part in the skills practice sessions, please let your instructor know so that accommodations can be made. If you are unable to participate fully in the course, you may "audit" the course and participate as much as you can or desire. In order to audit a course, you must let the instructor know before the training begins. Be aware that you will *not* be eligible to receive a course completion certificate.

PREVENTING EMERGENCIES

- Preventing emergencies is better than providing the best care if they do occur.
- Many emergencies result from unsafe actions or behaviors.
- Most emergencies that result from unsafe actions or behaviors are preventable.
- Recognizing the need for change is the first step in changing unsafe behaviors.
- Basic principles of injury prevention apply in all sports.
- Some sudden illnesses can also be prevented by controlling risk factors.
- Additional injury prevention practices may apply to specific sports.
- Coaches are most often in the best position to prevent injuries because they are responsible for the conduct of athletes and the training or competition session.

See Part 1 in the Sport Safety Training Handbook p. 2 for additional information on injury prevention.

Good Samaritan Laws

All states have enacted Good Samaritan laws to protect people who provide emergency care. These laws, which differ from state to state, may protect you from legal liability as long as you act in good faith, are not negligent and act within the scope of your training. You should contact a legal professional, your state attorney general's office or the local library to find out how your state's Good Samaritan laws affect your provision of emergency care in your athletic leadership role.

Obtaining Consent

You must get permission to help a conscious athlete.

- If a victim refuses care, at least call 9-1-1 or the local emergency number.
- You should be familiar with your sports organization's policies regarding permission to give care to minors in non–life-threatening situations.
- If the victim is a minor, a parent or guardian should be notified as soon as possible.
- Obtaining consent for a child in a life-threatening situation means that the parent or guardian would agree to give care if he or she could.

If a victim is unconscious, permission is implied.

To get consent:

- State your name;
- Tell the victim you are trained in first aid;
- Ask the victim if you can help;
- Explain what you think may be wrong; and
- Explain what you plan to do.

Preventing Disease Transmission

- The risk of getting a disease while giving first aid is extremely low, and taking basic precautions can reduce that risk even further.
- The term "**standard precautions**" refers to safety measures taken to prevent exposure to blood and body fluids when providing care to injured or ill persons. This approach to infection control means that you should consider **all** body fluids and substances as infectious. These precautions and practices include personal hygiene, using personal protective equipment, work practice controls, and equipment for cleaning and disinfection of contaminated surfaces. Whenever possible you should:
  - Avoid contact with blood and other body fluids or touching objects that may be soiled with blood or other body fluids.
  - Use alcohol-based hand rubs to clean your hands where handwashing facilities are not available, but not in place of handwashing with soap and water.
  - Wear protective clothing, such as disposable gloves, to cover any cuts, scrapes, and skin conditions you may have.
  - Wash your hands with soap and water immediately after giving care.
  - Place barriers, such as protective eyewear, CPR breathing barriers, and disposable gloves (latex or non-latex such as vinyl or nitrile) between you and an athlete's blood or other body fluids.
  - Remove jewelry such as rings and watches before providing care.
  - Avoid eating, drinking, smoking, applying cosmetics or lip balm, handling contact lenses or touching your mouth, nose, or eyes when you may be exposed to infectious materials or giving first aid.
- The steps for cleaning up blood and other body fluid spills are listed on p. 46 of the handbook.
- Gloves soiled with blood are considered contaminated and a biohazard and they should be disposed of properly.
- Remember to always give first aid care in ways that protect you and the injured person from disease transmission.
- Be prepared by always having a properly equipped first aid kit nearby.
- To learn more about reducing your risk of disease transmission, consider enrolling in an American Red Cross *Bloodborne Pathogens Training: Preventing Disease Transmission Course.*

TAKING ACTION

Your Role in the Emergency Medical Services (EMS) System

- *Recognize* that an emergency exists.
  - Signals of injury or sudden illness
  - Unusual noises, sights or odors
  - Unusual appearance or behavior
- *Decide* to act.
  - Hesitancy to act may be caused by fear of catching disease or fear of doing something wrong. BUT:
  - You are prepared;
  - You hold a position of authority;
  - You are expected to act; and
  - If not you, who?
- *Call 9-1-1* or the local emergency number for help.
- *Provide* care until help arrives.

THE EMERGENCY ACTION STEPS

- In any emergency, follow the emergency action steps:
  1. *CHECK* the scene for safety; check the injured or ill athlete.
  2. *CALL* 9-1-1 or the local emergency number when appropriate.
  3. *CARE* for the injured or ill athlete.
- Following these steps can minimize the confusion at an emergency scene.

CHECK

Answer these questions:

- Is the scene safe?
- What happened?
- Is there more than one injured or ill athlete?
- Can bystanders on the scene help?

CALL

Call 9-1-1 or the local emergency number if the injured or ill athlete—

- Is not breathing.
- Shows no signs of circulation.
- Is or becomes unconscious.
- Has breathing difficulty or is breathing irregularly.
- Has chest pain or pressure that lasts more than 3–5 minutes, or goes away and comes back.
- Is bleeding severely.
- Has pressure or pain in the abdomen that does not go away.
- Is vomiting blood or passing blood.
- Has seizures, a severe headache, or slurred speech.
- Appears to have been poisoned.
- Has injuries to the head, neck, or back.
- Has possible broken bones.

Also call for any of these situations:

- Fire or explosion;
- Downed electrical wires;
- Swiftly moving or rapidly rising water;
- Presence of poisonous gas;
- Vehicle collisions; or
- Injured or ill athlete who cannot be moved easily.

How to Activate the EMS System

- Call 9-1-1 or the local emergency number.
  - You may have to dial "9" or another digit to access an outside line.
- Give the dispatcher the information he or she requests. Most dispatchers will request the following information:
  - Location
  - Number you are calling from
  - Your name
  - What happened
  - Who is involved
  - Injured person's condition
  - Care being given
- Stay on the line until the dispatcher hangs up.
- Return to and care for the injured or ill athlete.

If you are ALONE—

Call FIRST—(before providing care) if an athlete is unconscious and over age 8 **OR** unconscious, under age 8 with *known* heart problems.

Call FAST—provide 1 minute of care (before making the call) if the athlete is unconscious and under age 8, a drowning/submersion victim, suffers cardiac arrest due to trauma or is a drug overdose victim.

- If you are alone and caring for a child (ages 1-8) with no signs of circulation, *Call FAST* applies; giving one minute of CPR is recommended before taking other actions, such as calling EMS or attaching an AED.

Care

Always keep a well-stocked first aid kit on hand *(see the Sport Safety Training Handbook p. xxi)*. They may be available from your local Red Cross Chapter.

- If necessary, send someone to call EMS personnel.
- Care for life-threatening emergencies.
- Watch for changes in breathing and consciousness.
- Help the athlete rest comfortably.
- To minimize shock, keep the athlete from getting chilled or overheated.
- Reassure the athlete.

ACTIVITIES

FILL-IN-THE-BLANKS

Write your answers in the blank spaces.

1. Generally the single most important action in an emergency is to____________________.
2. The worst thing you can do in an emergency is to _____________.
3. Your role in the EMS system includes four basic steps:
   ____
   ____
   ____
   ____
   ____
4. List the three steps to take in any emergency:
   ____
   ____
   ____
   ____
   ____

MULTIPLE CHOICE

Circle the answer or answers that correctly complete the following statements.

1. Standard precautions are safety measures you can take which include—(circle all that apply)
   a. Calling 9-1-1 or local emergency number.
   b. Not washing hands immediately after giving care.
   c. Avoiding objects soiled with blood or other body fluids.
   d. Using personal protective equipment such as CPR breathing barriers and disposable gloves.
2. Signals of life-threatening injuries include—(circle all that apply)
   a. Severe bleeding.
   b. No breathing.
   c. Breathing difficulty.
   d. No signs of circulation.
3. While waiting for EMS personnel, you should—(circle all that apply)
   a. Remove perspiration-soaked clothing.
   b. Reassure the athlete.
   c. Watch for changes in breathing and consciousness.
   d. All of the above.

TRUE/FALSE

Circle T if the statement is true; circle F if it is false.

1. **T F** If a scene is unsafe, tell bystanders to step back and carefully approach the athlete.
2. **T F** After checking the scene, the next thing to check is if the athlete is conscious.
3. **T F** Unconsciousness is not life-threatening.

BASIC RESPONSE STEPS FOR ANY EMERGENCY

Put the following steps in correct order for responding to an emergency involving an adult athlete. Write 1 in front of the first step to perform, 2 in front of the second step to perform, etc.

____ Give care to the injured athlete.
____ Check the scene for safety; check the injured athlete.
____ Call 9-1-1 or the local emergency number, if necessary.

SCENARIOS

Imagine yourself as the coach in the following situations. You have a first aid kit and your *Sport Safety Training Handbook*. Use your *Handbook* to answer the questions for this scenario, along with information you have learned in this course. Think about what you should do in the following situations.

1. After practice, one of your young gymnasts runs up to you and tells you another gymnast has passed out after wandering into a supply room down the hall from the locker room. What would you do first?
   ____
   ____
   ____
   ____
   ____
   ____
2. On the sidelines at a track meet, you see the father of one of your runners grasp his chest and suddenly collapse to the ground. He does not appear to be breathing. What would you do?
   ____
   ____
   ____
   ____
   ____
   ____
3. At the start of practice, one of your soccer players says he has been feeling an unusual "tightness" in his chest for several hours. Suddenly he

feels a severe chest pain and seems to be having breathing difficulty. What would you do?

____

____

____

____

____

____

4. The pitcher on your baseball team has been struck in the ankle by a line drive. He falls to the ground in pain and is unable to move his foot. What would you do?

____

____

____

____

____

____

ANSWERS TO ACTIVITIES

FILL-IN-THE-BLANKS

1. Call 9-1-1 or the local emergency number.
2. Do nothing.
3. Recognize the emergency.
   Decide to act.
   Call 9-1-1 or the local emergency number.
   Provide care.
4. Check the scene for safety and check the injured athlete.
   Call for help when appropriate.
   Care for the athlete until help arrives.

MULTIPLE CHOICE

1. **c and d are correct** (Avoiding objects soiled with blood or body fluids and using protective barriers reduces the risk of disease transmission.)
2. **a, b, c, and d are all correct** (All these may signal a life-threatening condition requiring immediate assistance from EMS personnel.)
3. **b and c are correct** (Reassuring the athlete helps him or her stay calm and can minimize shock; always watch for changes in breathing or consciousness that may signal the athlete's condition is worsening.)

TRUE/FALSE

1. **F** (Do not enter an unsafe scene.)
2. **T** (An athlete who is conscious and can speak is breathing and has a heartbeat; check first for consciousness, then for breathing and pulse.)
3. **F** (Unconsciousness is considered life threatening.)

STEPS OF FIRST AID

The steps should be numbered in this order:
3 Care
1 Check
2 Call

SCENARIOS

1. The scene may be unsafe—a gas or other substance in the supply room may be responsible for the gymnast becoming unconscious. If possible, remove her from the room immediately if she has no injury preventing her from being moved.

Note: This injury might have been prevented by checking the area for risk factors—the unlocked door should have been locked.

2. Check the injured or ill person. If he is unconscious, call 9-1-1 or the local emergency number immediately.
3. Check the athlete. This is a life-threatening emergency. Call 9-1-1 or the local emergency number immediately.

Note: This athlete may be having a heart attack as a result of cardiovascular disease. Some cardiovascular disease may be prevented by modifying personal risk factors (see Lesson 5) and receiving annual medical examinations that would detect cardiovascular disease.

4. Check the athlete. This is not a life-threatening emergency, but you may still need to call 9-1-1 or the local emergency number. In the meantime, you should care for the injury.

2

LESSON

CHECKING AN INJURED OR ILL ATHLETE

2 LESSON CHECKING AN INJURED OR ILL ATHLETE

- *Checking* the scene for safety and checking an injured or ill athlete is the first action to take, followed by *calling* for help when appropriate and then *caring* for the athlete.
  - **When to Move an Injured or Ill Athlete—**
    1. When faced with immediate danger
    2. To reach another person with a more serious injury
    3. To provide proper care
- The process of checking the athlete depends on whether the athlete is conscious or unconscious, adult or child.
- For this course, an "adult" is defined as someone who is 9 years old or older and a "child" is defined as someone 1 to 8 years old.

CHECKING AN UNCONSCIOUS ATHLETE—ADULT OR CHILD

Check if the athlete is conscious. *If the athlete does not respond, assume he or she is unconscious and send someone to call 9-1-1 or the local emergency number.* If no one is available to call, make the call yourself before starting any care.

If the injured or ill athlete is a child, provide 1 minute of care before making the call.

- **Check if an unconscious athlete—**

- Is breathing.
- Shows signs of circulation *(look for: normal breathing, coughing or movement in response to rescue breaths or a pulse).*
- Is bleeding severely.

In the following lessons, you will learn the emergency care for an injured or ill athlete who is not breathing, who does not have a pulse, or who is bleeding severely.

SKILL PRACTICE

Use the skill sheet on the following pages to guide your practice of the skill of checking an unconscious athlete.

CHECKING AN UNCONSCIOUS ATHLETE—ADULT OR CHILD

***CHECK** the scene for safety. **CHECK** the injured athlete, following standard precautions. To **CHECK** an athlete—*

1 STEP

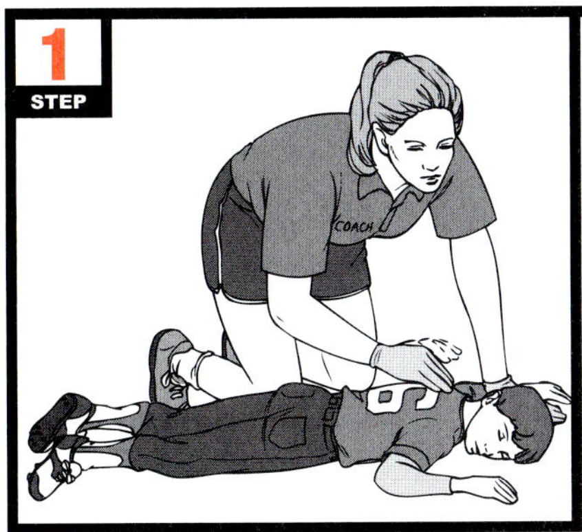

Tap and shout to see if the athlete responds.

If no response, call 9-1-1 or the local emergency number.

For a child, give care for 1 minute, and then call 9-1-1 or the local emergency number.

2 STEP

If the athlete is face-down, look, listen and feel for breathing for about 5 seconds. If the athlete is face-up, go to step 4.

If athlete is not breathing or you cannot tell—

3 STEP

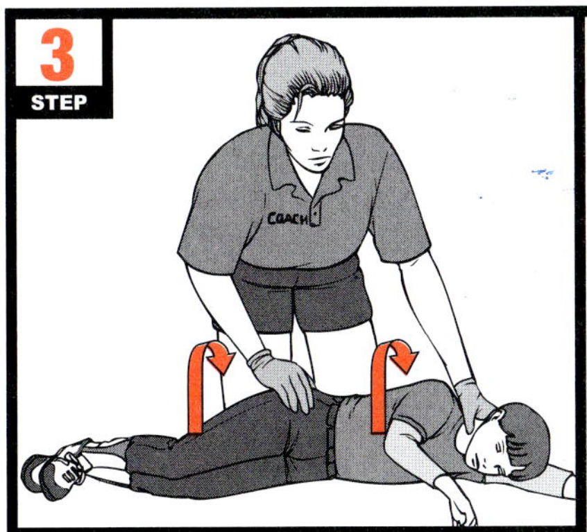

Position the athlete on his or her back, while supporting the head, neck and back.

Continued on next page.

SKILL SHEET

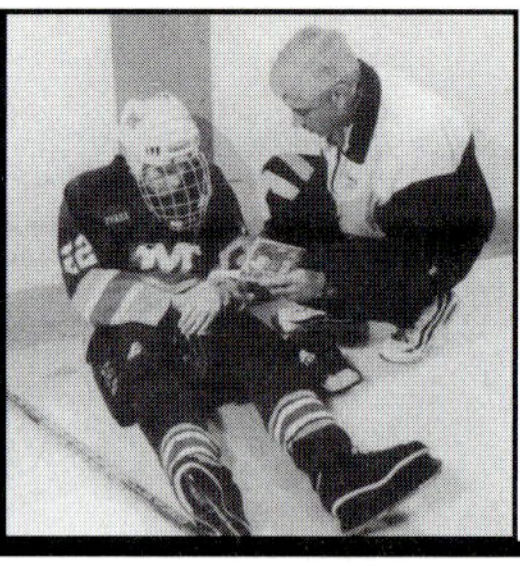

CHECKING AN UNCONSCIOUS ATHLETE—ADULT OR CHILD

4 STEP

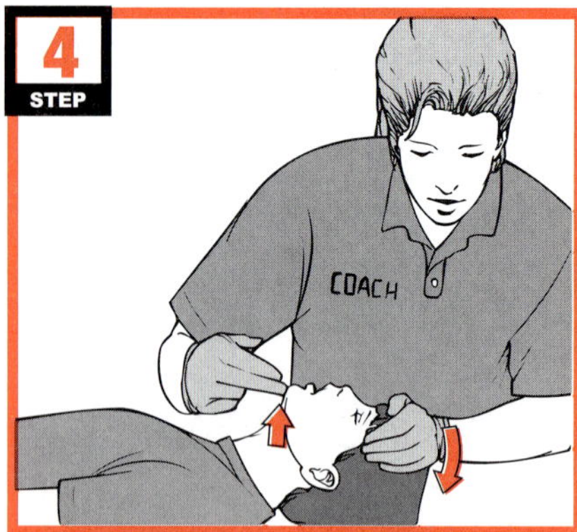

Tilt the head back and lift the chin.

With a child, do not tilt the head back as far.

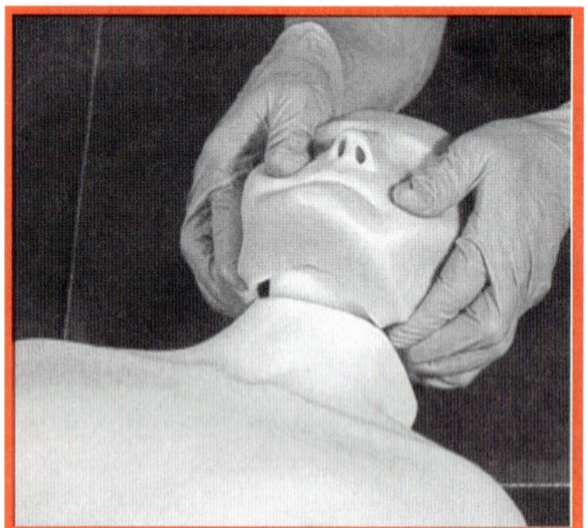

Note: If you suspect a head, neck or back injury, use the jaw thrust maneuver to open the airway. Minimize movement of the head and neck when opening the airway.

5 STEP

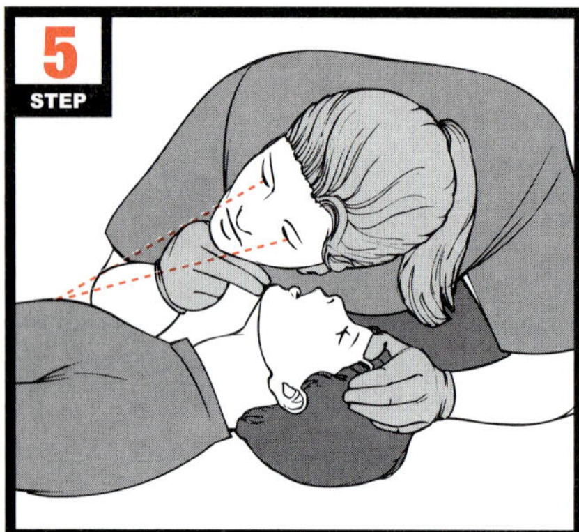

Look, listen and feel for breathing for about 5 seconds.

CHECKING AN UNCONSCIOUS ATHLETE—ADULT OR CHILD

6 STEP

With the athlete's head tilted back and chin lifted, pinch the nose shut.

With a child, do not tilt the head back as far.

Give 2 slow breaths. Breathe into the athlete until the chest clearly rises.

7 STEP

Check for signs of circulation (normal breathing, coughing or movement in response to rescue breaths or a pulse) for no more than 10 seconds.

8 STEP

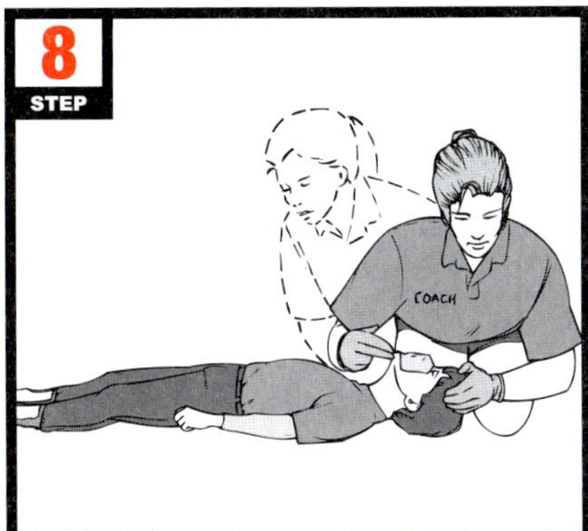

Check for severe bleeding.

Give care for the conditions you find.

9 STEP

If athlete is unconscious, breathing normally and has no suspected head, neck or back injury, place in a recovery position.

SKILL SHEET

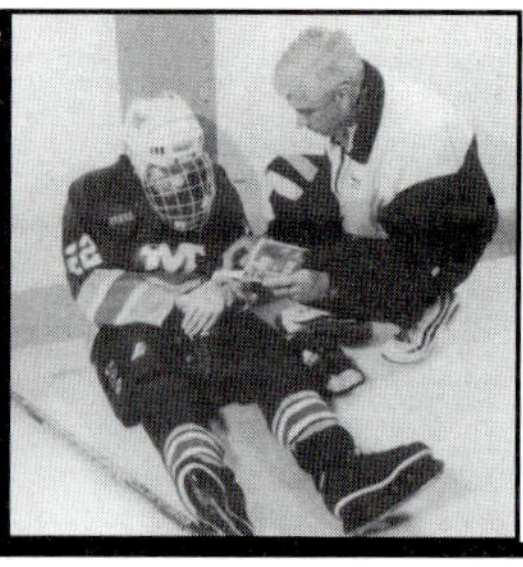

REMOVING DISPOSABLE GLOVES

1 STEP

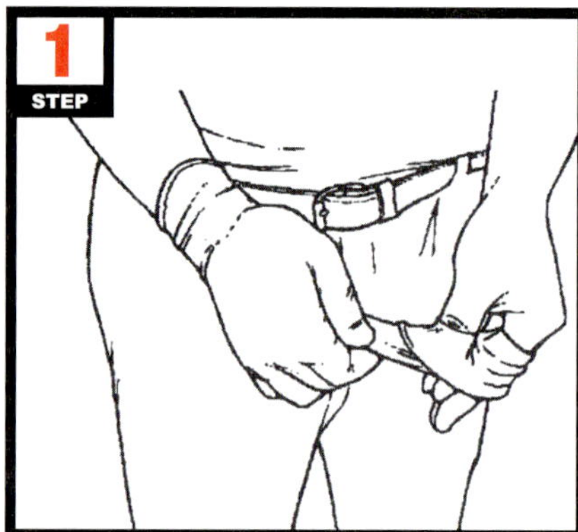

Partially Remove First Glove—

Pinch glove at the wrist, being careful to touch only the glove's outside surface.

Pull glove toward the fingertips without completely removing it.

The glove is now inside out.

2 STEP

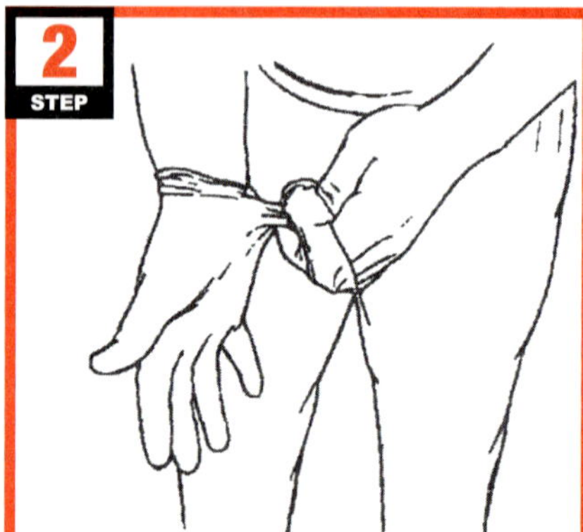

Remove Second Glove—

With partially gloved hand, pinch the exterior of second glove.

Pull the second glove toward the fingertips until it is inside out, then remove it completely.

SKILL SHEET

REMOVING DISPOSABLE GLOVES

3 STEP

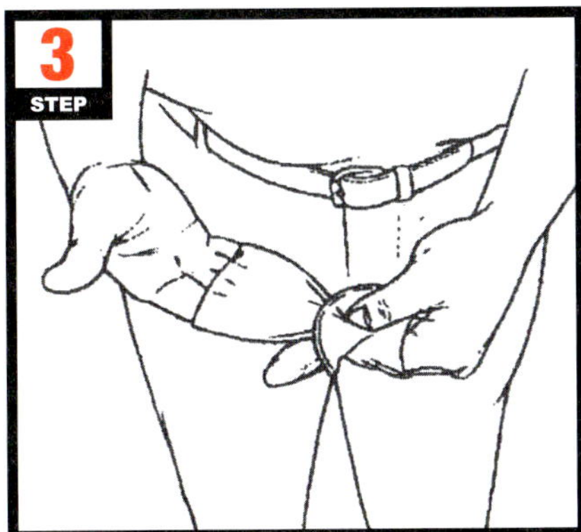

Finish Removing Both Gloves—

Grasp both gloves with your free hand.

Touch only the clean interior surface of the glove.

4 STEP

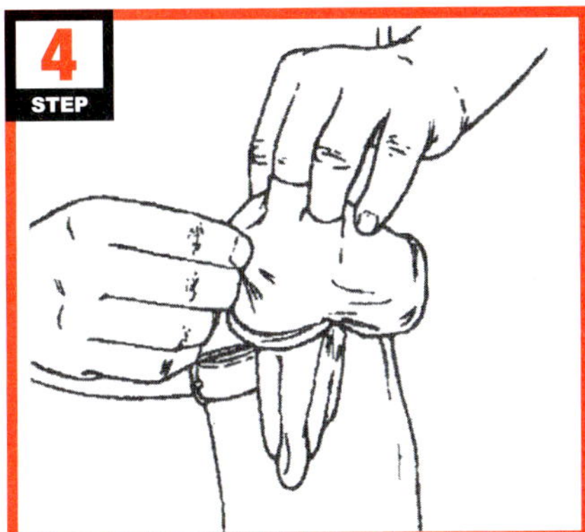

After Removing Both Gloves—

Discard gloves in an appropriate container.

Wash your hands thoroughly.

CARING FOR SHOCK

- Shock is a life-threatening condition in which not enough blood is being delivered to all parts of the body.
- An athlete going into shock needs immediate medical attention.
- Body systems and organs begin to fail.
- Shock may be caused by severe bleeding, serious internal injury, significant fluid loss or other conditions.
- The goals of first aid are to get help quickly and give care to minimize shock while caring for the injury or illness.

See the Sport Safety Training Handbook, p. 159, for signals of and how to care for shock.

CHECKING A CONSCIOUS ATHLETE—ADULT

For this course, "adult" is defined as someone who is 9 years old or older.
Check a conscious adult athlete by—

- Talking to the athlete and to bystanders to find out what happened.
- Checking the athlete from head to toe (obtain consent first).

Do not ask the athlete to move or move the athlete yourself.

CHECKING A CONSCIOUS ATHLETE—CHILD

For this course, a "child" is defined as someone 1 to 8 years old.

- The process is similar to checking a conscious adult, except your check of the body proceeds from *toe to head.*
  - Talk to the child and to bystanders to find out what happened.
  - Check the child from *toe to head.*
- Do not ask the athlete to move or move the athlete yourself.
- Checking a younger athlete can be more challenging because of emotional and communication differences.
- Follow these guidelines:
  1. Observe the athlete for signals of injury or illness before touching him or her.
  2. Remain calm to help keep the athlete and parent or guardian calm.
  3. Communicate clearly with the parent or guardian and the athlete; talk slowly and use simple words.
  4. Do not separate the child from the parent or guardian unless necessary.
  5. Gain trust through your actions.
  6. Be at eye level with the child.

SKILL SHEET

CHECKING THE CONSCIOUS ATHLETE—ADULT OR CHILD

CHECK *the scene for safety,* **CHECK** *the injured athlete, following standard precautions as appropriate. To check an athlete—*

1 STEP Talk to the athlete or bystanders to find out what happened.

2 STEP Get consent to give care—

- State your name.
- Tell the athlete you are trained in first aid.
- Ask the athlete if you can help.
- Explain what you think may be wrong.
- Explain what you plan to do.

3 STEP Check the athlete from head to toe.

- Check a child from toe, to head and be aware of emotional and communication differences with a younger athlete.
- Stay at eye level with an athlete.
- Do not separate an athlete from the parent or guardian.

Do not ask the athlete to move or move the athlete yourself, unless there is an *immediate danger* to you or the athlete.

Continued on next page.

SKILL SHEET

CHECKING THE CONSCIOUS ATHLETE—ADULT OR CHILD

STEP 4 Care for the athlete based on the conditions found.

- Care for life-threatening conditions first.
- Take steps to minimize the effects of shock

STEP 5 Continue to monitor the athlete's ABC's—airway, breathing and circulation.

If EMS is called—

STEP 6 Give information about the child's condition and about what care has been given to EMS personnel when they arrive.

ACTIVITIES

TRUE/FALSE

Circle T if the statement is true; circle F if it is false.

1. **T F** If an athlete is not breathing, then his or her heart is not beating.
2. **T F** If an athlete is not breathing, his or her life is in danger.
3. **T F** If an athlete is unconscious, send someone to call 9-1-1 or the local emergency number unless he or she is breathing.

STEPS IN CHECKING AN UNCONSCIOUS ATHLETE

Put the following steps in correct order for checking an unconscious athlete. Write 1 in front of the first step to perform, 2 in front of the second step, etc.

____ Check for bleeding.
____ Check for signs of circulation.
____ Check breathing.

MULTIPLE CHOICE

Circle the answer or answers that correctly complete the following statements.

1. An athlete who is able to talk—
   a. Is breathing.
   b. Shows signs of circulation.
   c. Does not have life-threatening injuries.
   d. Does not have a head, neck or back injury.
2. When checking an athlete for problems—
   a. Ask him or her to sit up so that you can check more effectively.
   b. Help the athlete move body parts that hurt.
   c. Look for medical alert tags. Be aware that, in some sports, athletes are not allowed to wear medical alert tags.
   d. Check how the skin looks and feels.
3. A basketball player is elbowed to the head and drops to the floor. When you reach the injured player, you hear her softly crying in pain. What do you know about her level of consciousness?
   a. She is unconscious.
   b. She is conscious.
   c. You are not sure yet.

ANSWERS TO ACTIVITIES

TRUE/FALSE

1. F (An injured or ill athlete may still have a pulse even though breathing has stopped; this athlete needs rescue breathing. Unless the athlete gets oxygen soon, however, the heart will soon stop and CPR will be necessary.)
2. T (Because an athlete cannot live long without oxygen, not breathing is a life-threatening condition.)
3. F (Whenever an athlete is unconscious, always send someone to call 9-1-1 or the local emergency number, because the athlete's condition may be life threatening.)

STEPS IN CHECKING AN UNCONSCIOUS ATHLETE

The steps given should be numbered in this order:
3 Check bleeding.
2 Check for signs of circulation.
1 Check breathing.

MULTIPLE CHOICE

1. **a and b are correct** (The ability to talk means the athlete is breathing and shows signs of circulation; yet the athlete may still have other life-threatening conditions.)
2. **c and d are correct** (Always check for medical alert tags and check the condition of the athlete's skin; *do not* move the athlete or ask the athlete to move body areas that hurt, because movement may worsen the injury.)
3. **b is correct** (An injured athlete who can talk or cry is conscious and therefore is breathing and shows signs of circulation.)

Note: Could this basketball injury have been prevented? Some sports injuries cannot be prevented. Others, possibly including this one, may have been prevented by coaching the players how to move safely in certain situations.

3
LESSON

BREATHING EMERGENCIES AND CONSCIOUS CHOKING ATHLETE

3 LESSON BREATHING EMERGENCIES AND CONSCIOUS CHOKING ATHLETE

BREATHING EMERGENCIES

- A breathing emergency occurs when an athlete is having breathing difficulty or cannot breathe.
- Choking is a breathing emergency.
- Breathing emergencies are life-threatening.
- First aid for breathing emergencies is basically the same for both adults and children.

Preventing Breathing Emergencies

- Many instances of choking can be prevented by not talking or running with food or objects in the mouth; children are particularly susceptible to choking.
- Breathing emergencies caused by asthma can usually be prevented by following the physician's guidelines and taking prescribed medication.
- Breathing emergencies caused by hyperventilation can also be prevented by avoiding unsafe practices, such as swimmers intentionally hyperventilating before swimming underwater.
- Breathing emergencies related to allergic reactions can be prevented by recognizing the first signals of an allergic reaction and getting help immediately (see Allergic Reactions in the *Sport Safety Training Handbook*, p. 72).
- Injury-related breathing emergencies may be prevented by following safe sports practices, such as using proper training methods and safe facilities.

See also Part 1 of the Sport Safety Training Handbook for additional safety practices.

Signals of Breathing Emergencies—

- The athlete is not breathing.
- The athlete is apprehensive or fearful.
- Breathing is *unusually* slow or rapid.
- Breaths are *unusually* deep or shallow.
- The athlete is *unusually* gasping for breath.
- The athlete is wheezing, gurgling, or making high-pitched noises.
- The athlete's skin is *unusually* moist.
- The athlete's skin has an *unusually* flushed, pale or ashen or bluish appearance.
- The athlete feels *unusually* short of breath.
- The athlete feels dizzy or lightheaded.
- The athlete feels pain in the chest or tingling in the hands or feet.

***See also p. 103 of the Sport Safety Training Handbook.* Some of these conditions can cause a person to stop breathing, that is why you need to know how to perform rescue breathing and will learn this skill in the next lesson.**

CHOKING—CONSCIOUS ATHLETE

If an athlete is conscious but cannot cough, speak or breathe, suspect that an object is blocking the airway and the athlete is choking.

First Aid for Choking—Conscious Athlete

See the Sport Safety Training Handbook p. 125 for Choking—Conscious Adult or Child Athlete.

SKILL PRACTICE

Use the skill sheet on the following pages to guide your practice of giving abdominal thrusts to a conscious athlete—adult or child.

SKILL SHEET

CONSCIOUS CHOKING ATHLETE

Never give abdominal thrusts to an athlete who is not choking!

CHECK the scene for safety. Check the injured athlete, following standard precautions as appropriate. If the athlete is unable to cough, speak, or breathe—

1 STEP

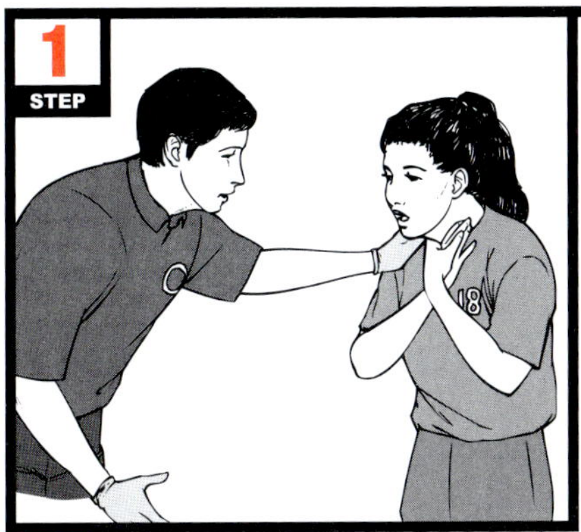

Obtain permission to give care.

2 STEP

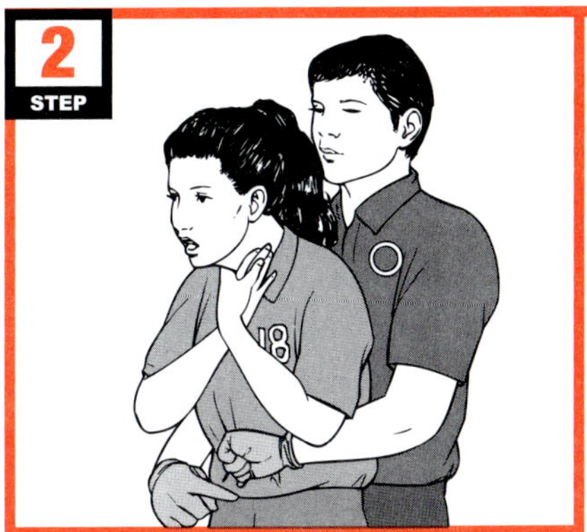

Place the thumb side of the fist against the middle of the abdomen just above the navel. Grasp the fist with the other hand.

- **For a child, stand or kneel behind the child, depending on his or her size.**

Continued on next page.

CONSCIOUS CHOKING ATHLETE

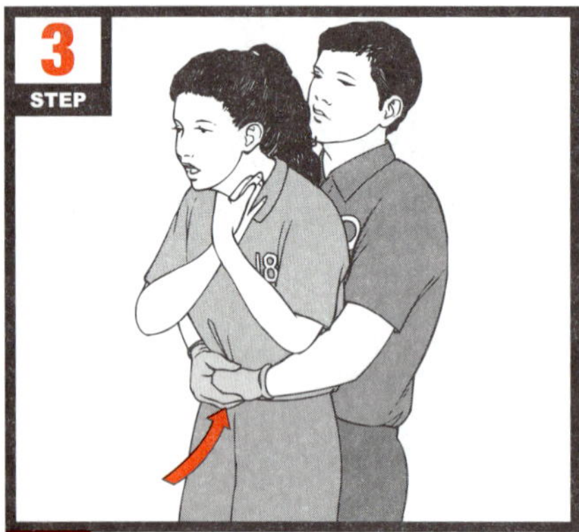

Give quick, upward thrusts. Repeat until—

- The object is expelled;
- The athlete starts to breathe or cough forcefully;
- The athlete becomes unconscious; or
- EMS personnel or another trained person takes over.

If the athlete becomes unconscious, follow the steps on p. 43.

ACTIVITIES

STEPS OF CARE—CONSCIOUS CHOKING ATHLETE (ADULT OR CHILD)

Put the following steps in correct order for giving abdominal thrusts to a conscious athlete. Write 1 in front of the first step to perform, 2 in front of the second, etc.

____ Place the thumb side of the fist against the middle of the abdomen just above the navel and grasp the fist with the other hand.

____ Position yourself behind the choking athlete.

____ Give quick, upward thrusts.

FILL-IN-THE-BLANKS

1. How does first aid for choking differ between a conscious adult and a conscious child?

   ____

   ____

2. You (should/should *not*) ______________ give abdominal thrusts to an athlete who is not choking.

MULTIPLE CHOICE

Circle the answer or answers that correctly complete the following statements.

1. Ways to prevent breathing emergencies include—
   a. not talking or running with food or objects in the mouth.
   b. avoiding unsafe practices, such as swimmers intentionally hyperventilating.
   c. following safe sports practices, such as using proper training methods and safe facilities.
   d. All of the above.
2. Signals of a breathing emergency include—
   a. unusually slow or rapid, deep or shallow breathing.
   b. wheezing, gurgling or making high-pitched noises.
   c. unusually dry, hot skin.
   d. Both a and b.

ANSWERS TO ACTIVITIES

STEPS OF CARE—CONSCIOUS CHOKING ATHLETE (ADULT OR CHILD)

The steps for giving abdominal thrusts to a conscious athlete should be numbered as follows:

2 Place the thumb side of the fist against the middle of the abdomen just above the navel and grasp the fist with the other hand

1 Position yourself behind the choking athlete.

3 Give quick, upward thrusts.

FILL-IN-THE-BLANKS

1. You may have to stand or kneel behind the child, depending on his or her size, but otherwise, the skill is the same.
2. Should *not*.

MULTIPLE CHOICE

1. **d is correct** (Many instances of choking can be prevented by not talking or running with food or objects in the mouth; breathing emergencies caused by hyperventilation can also be prevented by avoiding unsafe practices; injury-related breathing emergencies may be prevented by following safe sports practices.)
2. **d is correct** (Dry, hot skin is a signal of a late-stage heat-related emergency, sometimes called heat stroke).

4

LESSON

RESCUE BREATHING

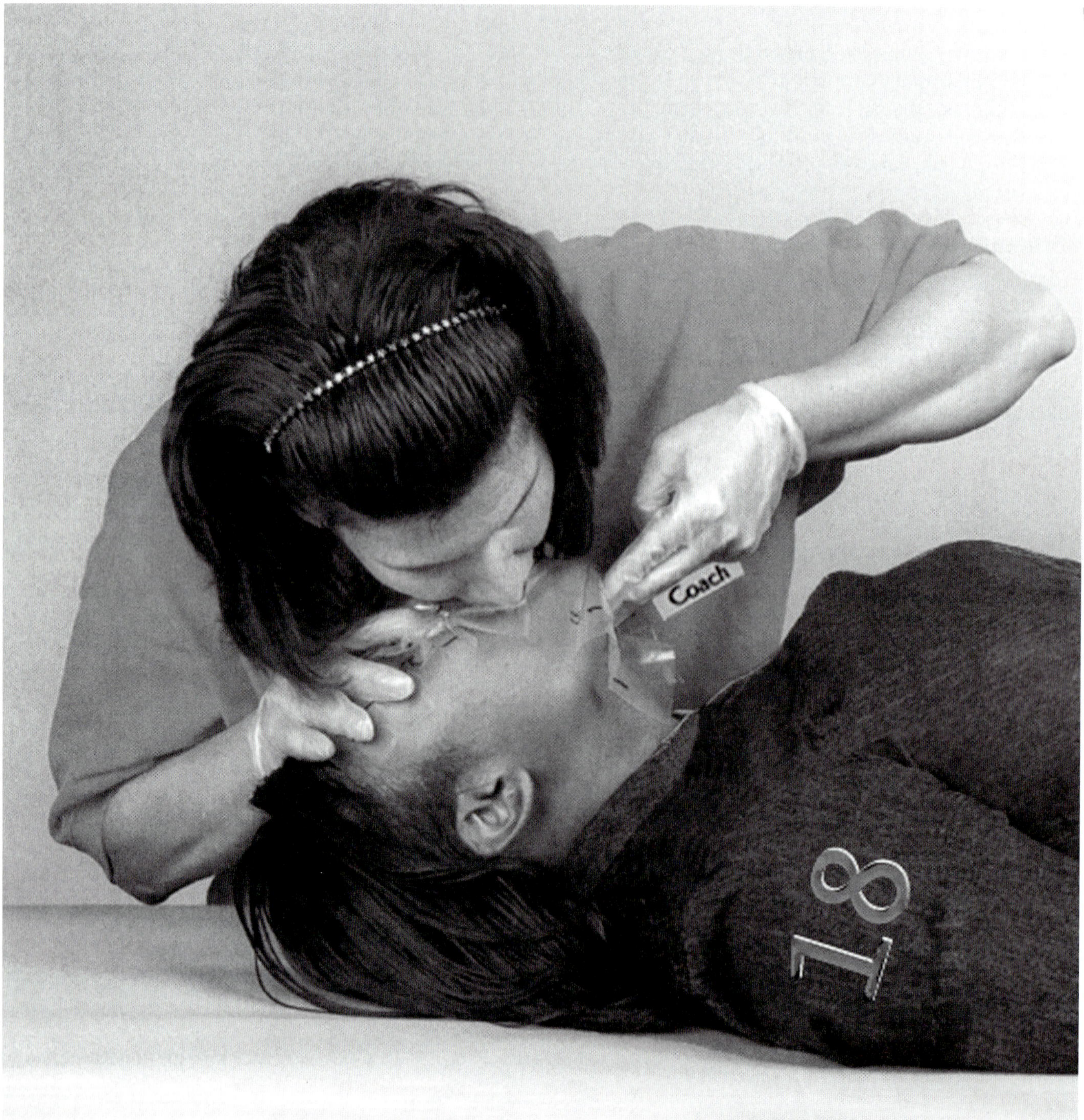

4
LESSON

RESCUE BREATHING

RESCUE BREATHING

- Rescue breathing is the process of breathing air into a non-breathing athlete.
- Rescue breaths should be slow and gentle and should make the chest clearly rise.
- It is natural to feel uncomfortable making mouth-to-mouth contact with someone, especially someone you do not know.
- The risk of transmission of a serious disease during rescue breathing is extremely low.

Breathing Barriers and Devices

- A resuscitation mask or face-shield (also known as a CPR breathing barrier) may reduce the risk of disease transmission between the rescuer and the athlete.
- A breathing barrier should be used whenever possible. However, a responder should not delay care if a breathing barrier is not immediately available or if he or she is unsure of how to use it.
- Be prepared: Have a resuscitation mask or face-shield in your first aid kit at the practice setting or athletic event.

Rescue Breathing

See Sport Safety Training Handbook p. 105 for Checking an Unconscious Athlete—Rescue Breathing—Adult or Child

SKILL SHEET

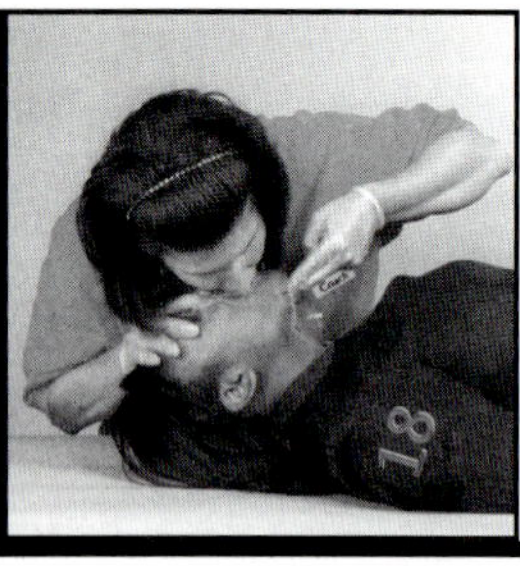

RESCUE BREATHING—ADULT OR CHILD

Complete "Checking an Unconscious Athlete—Adult or Child," pages 11-13.

CHECK ***the scene for safety.*** **CHECK** ***the injured athlete, following standard precautions. To determine if an athlete needs rescue breathing—***

STEP 1 **Tap and shout to see if the athlete responds. If no response, CALL 9-1-1 or the local emergency number.**

For a child, give care for 1 minute, and then call 9-1-1 or the local emergency number.

STEP 2 **If the athlete is face-down, look listen, and feel for breathing for about 5 seconds. If the athlete is face-up, go to step 4.**

If the athlete is not breathing or you cannot tell—

STEP 3 **Position the athlete on his or her back, while supporting the head, neck and back.**

STEP 4 **Tilt the head back and lift the chin.**

- **With a child, do not tilt the head back as far.**

STEP 5 **Look, listen and feel for breathing for about 5 seconds.**

SKILL SHEET

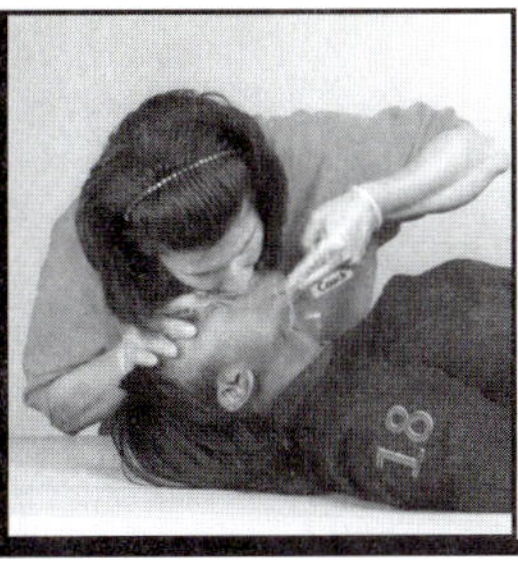

RESCUE BREATHING—ADULT OR CHILD

If the athlete is not breathing—

6 STEP

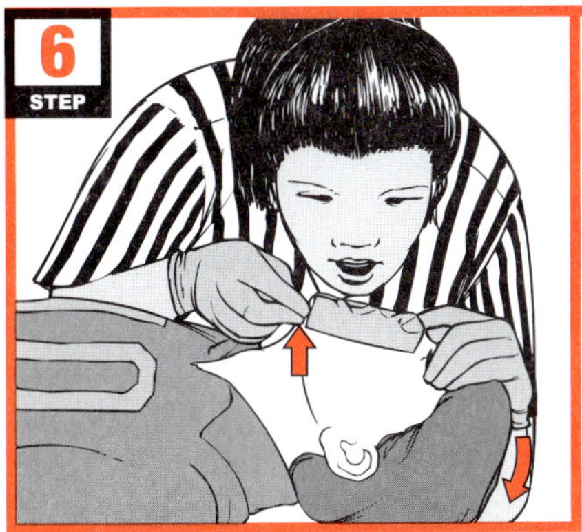

With the athlete's head tilted back and chin lifted. Pinch the nose shut.

7 STEP

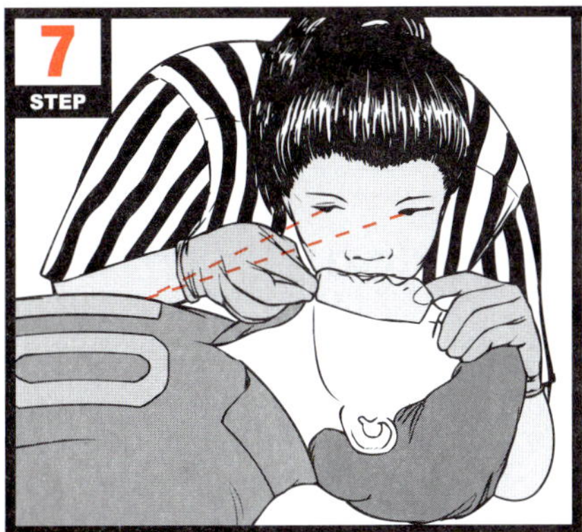

Give 2 slow breaths. Breathe into the athlete until the chest clearly rises.

8 STEP

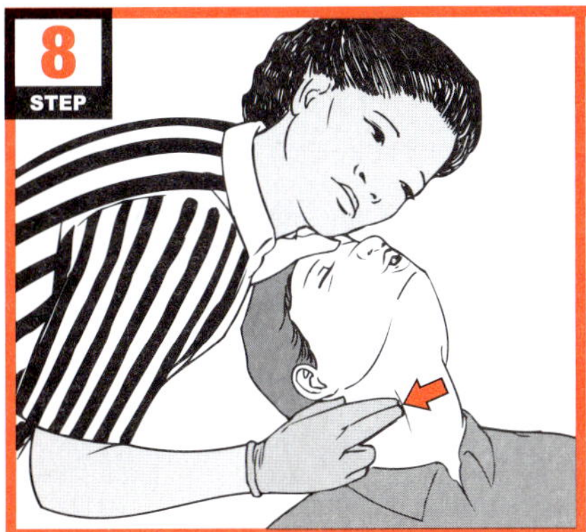

Check for signs of circulation: normal breathing, coughing or movement in response to rescue breaths or a pulse. Feel for a pulse at the groove in the side of the neck.

Continued on next page.

SKILL SHEET

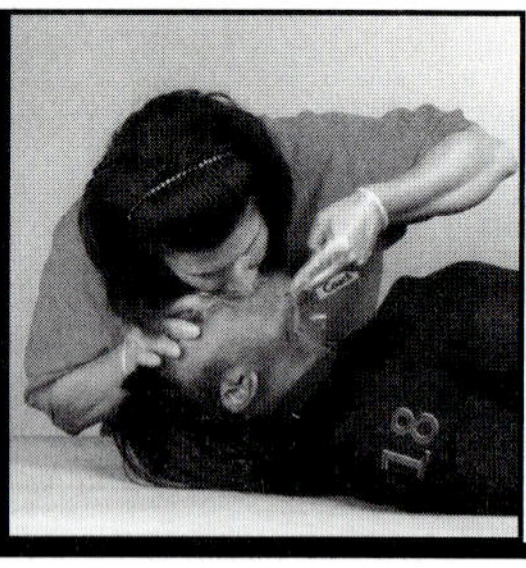

RESCUE BREATHING—ADULT OR CHILD

If a sign of circulation (such as coughing or movement in response to rescue breaths or a pulse) IS present but the athlete is still NOT breathing—

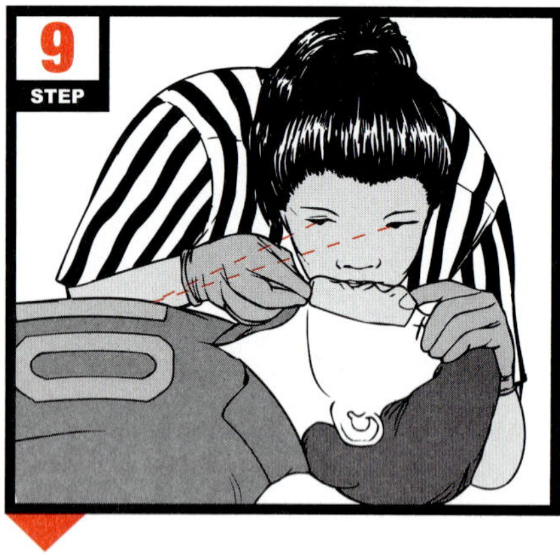

Give 1 slow rescue breath about every 5 seconds.

Do this for about 1 minute (12 breaths).

For a child (ages 1-8), give 1 rescue breath about every 3 seconds (about 20 breaths per minute).

Recheck for signs of circulation about every minute.

Continue rescue breathing as long as a pulse or other sign of circulation is present but the athlete is not breathing.

ACTIVITIES

STEPS FOR RESCUE BREATHING

Put the following steps in correct order for giving rescue breathing. Write 1 in front of the first step to perform, 2 in front of the second, etc.

____ Check for signs of circulation (such as coughing or movement in response to rescue breaths or a pulse).

____ If a sign of circulation is present but the athlete is not breathing, give 1 slow breath about every 5 seconds (adult)/3 seconds (child) for about 1 minute.

____ With the head tilted back and the chin lifted, pinch the nose shut.

____ Give 2 slow breaths, breathing in until the chest clearly rises.

____ Recheck signs of circulation about every minute.

FILL-IN-THE-BLANKS

What are the two ways that rescue breathing differs between an adult and a child?

____

____

____

____

SCENARIO

Imagine yourself as the coach in the following situation. You have a first aid kit and your *Sport Safety Training Handbook*. Use your *Handbook* to answer the question for this scenario, along with information you have learned in this course.

You walk in the locker room before volleyball practice and find a player unconscious on the floor. You see no blood or other signs of injury. After checking the scene for safety, the victim for consciousness and calling 9-1-1 or your local emergency number, what should you do?

____

____

____

____

____

____

ANSWERS TO ACTIVITIES

STEPS FOR RESCUE BREATHING

The steps for rescue breathing should be numbered as follows:

3 Check for a sign of circulation (such as coughing or movement in response to rescue breaths or a pulse).

4 If a sign of circulation is present but the athlete is not breathing, give 1 rescue breath about every 5 seconds (adult)/3 seconds (child) for about 1 minute.

1 With the head tilted back and the chin lifted, pinch the nose shut.

2 Give 2 rescue breaths, breathing in until the chest clearly rises.

5 Recheck signs of circulation about every minute.

FILL-IN-THE-BLANKS

The differences in rescue breathing for adult and child:

- Do not tilt a child's head back as far as an adult when opening the airway.
- If a sign of circulation is present but the athlete is still not breathing, give 1 rescue breath about every 5 seconds for an adult and 1 rescue breath about every 3 seconds for a child.

SCENARIO

High School Volleyball Team

- Open the airway and check for breathing.
- If you determine that he is not breathing, attempt 2 rescue breaths.
- If the chest clearly rises, check for signs of circulation.
- If you find signs of circulation, but the athlete is still not breathing, perform rescue breathing.
  - Give 1 rescue breath about every 5 seconds.
- Recheck for breathing and signs of circulation after one minute and continue rescue breathing, until the athlete starts breathing on his own, or EMS personnel arrive and take over.

5

LESSON

THE CARDIAC CHAIN-OF-SURVIVAL AND CARDIAC EMERGENCIES

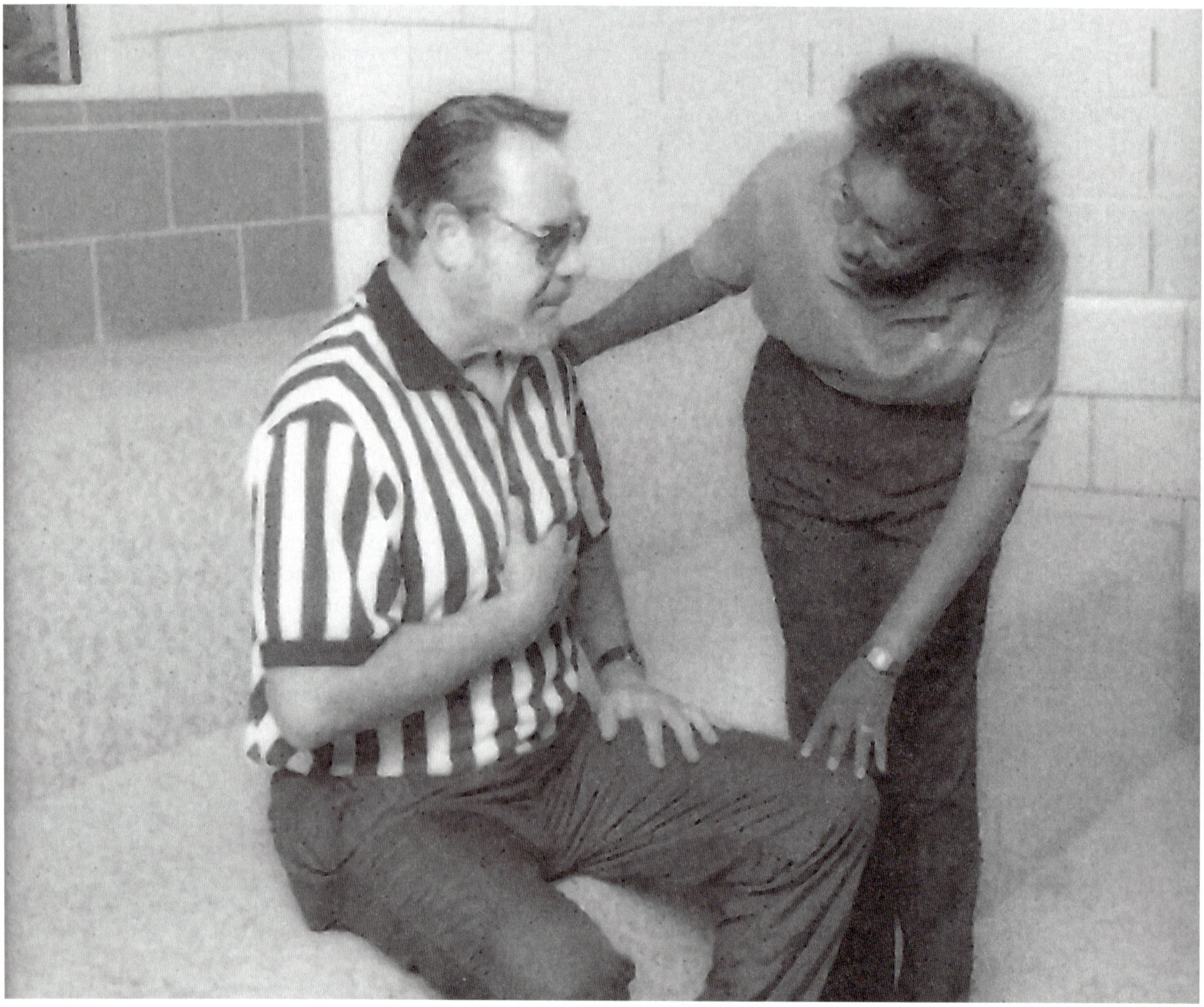

5 LESSON THE CARDIAC CHAIN-OF-SURVIVAL AND CARDIAC EMERGENCIES

See the Sport Safety Training Handbook p. 123 for Chest Pain or Pressure/Possible Heart Attack.

THE CARDIAC CHAIN OF SURVIVAL

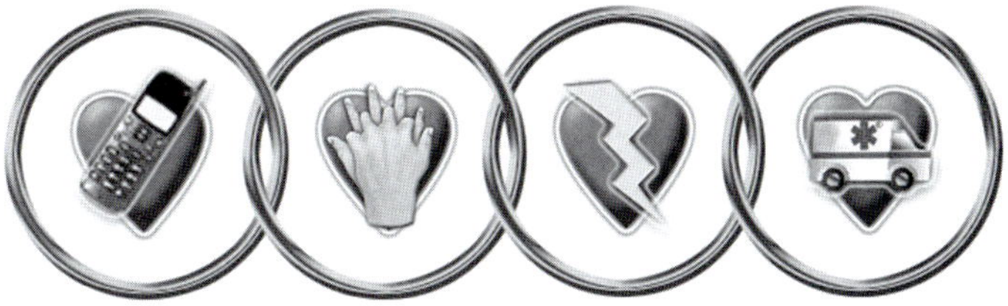

Early recognition and early access | Early CPR | Early defibrillation | Early advanced medical care

CPR alone is not enough to help someone survive a cardiac arrest. Emergency medical care is needed as soon as possible. This is why it is so important to call 9-1-1 or the local emergency number immediately. The greatest chance of survival from cardiac arrest occurs when the following sequence of events happens as rapidly as possible:

1. **Early recognition and early access.** The sooner 9-1-1 or your workplace emergency number is called; the sooner early advanced life support arrives.
2. **Early CPR.** Early CPR helps circulate blood that contains oxygen to the vital organs until an AED is ready to use or advanced medical personnel arrive.
3. **Early defibrillation.** Most victims of sudden cardiac arrest need an electric shock called defibrillation. Each minute that defibrillation is delayed reduces the chance of survival by about 10 percent.
4. **Early advanced medical care.** This is given by trained medical personnel who provide further care and transport to hospital facilities.

RECOGNIZING A HEART ATTACK

Heart Attack—

- A heart attack occurs when the heart does not receive enough blood and oxygen to function properly.
- Cardiac arrest, a condition where the heart completely stops functioning altogether or functions too poorly to circulate blood can *result* from a heart attack.
- Many lives are lost because people deny that they are having a heart attack and delay calling for help.
- Recognizing the signals of a heart attack and calling EMS personnel before the heart stops are critical elements in saving lives.
- Act quickly if a person is experiencing any of the signals of a heart attack. Call 9-1-1 or the local emergency number right away.

Signals of a Heart Attack—

- Persistent chest pain or pressure (a primary signal of a heart attack) that lasts longer than 3-5 minutes, or goes away and comes back;
- Chest pain spreading to the shoulders, neck, jaw or arms;
- Shortness of breath or trouble breathing;
- Nausea or vomiting;
- Dizziness, lightheadedness or fainting;
- Pale, ashen (grayish) or bluish skin;

- Sweating; and
- Denial.
- As with a man, a woman's most common heart attack symptom is chest pain or discomfort. But women are somewhat more likely to experience some of the other warning signs, particularly shortness of breath, nausea, vomiting and back or jaw pain.

Care for a Heart Attack—

- Follow standard precautions.
- Recognize the signals of a heart attack.
- Call or have someone call 9-1-1 or the local emergency number.
- Convince the person to stop activity and rest.
- Help the person to rest comfortably.
- Try to obtain information about the person's condition.
- Comfort the person.
- Assist with medication, if prescribed.
- Monitor the person's condition.
- Be prepared to give CPR if the person's heart stops beating and use an AED if one is available and you are trained.

Cardiovascular Disease—

- Heart disease, or cardiovascular disease, is the leading killer of people in the United States.

Guidelines for a Heart-Healthy Lifestyle—

1. Eat a balanced diet that limits intake of saturated fat and cholesterol.
2. Participate in continuous, vigorous physical activity for 20 to 30 minutes or more at least three times a week.
3. Have blood pressure and cholesterol levels checked regularly.
4. Maintain appropriate weight.
5. Have a physical examination before the start of every season of athletic training or competition.

ACTIVITIES

FILL-IN-THE-BLANKS

1. What is a common signal of a heart attack?

____

____

2. What are three other signals of a heart attack?

____

____

____

____

____

____

3. What are five lifestyle factors associated with an increased incidence of cardiovascular disease?

____

____

____

____

____

MULTIPLE CHOICE

Circle the answer or answers that correctly complete the following statements.

1. Which of the following actions are immediate care steps for a person who may be experiencing a heart attack?
   a. Give rescue breathing.
   b. Call or send someone to call 9-1-1 or the local emergency number.
   c. Help the person rest comfortably.
   d. Have the person lie on his or her back, with feet raised 8-12 inches.
   e. Give CPR and use an AED.
2. Persons experiencing a heart attack often do not get timely help because—
   a. They confuse heart attack signals with muscle soreness.
   b. They believe they have indigestion.
   c. Others fail to recognize the key signals of heart attack.
   d. All of the above.
3. EMS personnel should be called for a person experiencing persistent chest pain or discomfort if the pain does not go away—
   a. In an hour.
   b. Overnight.
   c. After bed rest.
   d. In 3 to 5 minutes.
   e. In 30 minutes.
4. If you suspect a person is having a heart attack, the *first* thing you should do is—
   a. Send someone to call EMS personnel.
   b. Assist with medication, if prescribed.
   c. Have the person stop whatever he or she is doing and rest.
   d. Find out medical information about the person.
5. Exercise that builds up cardiovascular fitness also can help people—
   a. Cope with stress.
   b. Reduce infections.
   c. Control weight.
   d. Sleep better.
6. Programs to control or lose weight—
   a. Are not an issue.
   b. Should include exercise.
   c. Generally allow you to eat whatever you want.
   d. All of the above.

TRUE/FALSE

Circle T if the statement is true; circle F if it is false.

1. **T F** Cardiac arrest is another term for heart attack.
2. **T F** Persistent chest pain or pressure can signal a life-threatening condition.
3. **T F** Many people having a heart attack find it easier to breathe while lying on their backs.
4. **T F** Heart disease is the primary cause of cardiac arrest.
5. **T F** A personal program to prevent heart disease must begin when a person is young to have any meaningful effect.
6. **T F** Multiple risk factors increase the chance of having a heart attack.
7. **T F** Heart disease develops slowly.
8. **T F** Personal programs to prevent heart disease should begin in the adult years.
9. **T F** After a few years, a person who quits smoking enjoys the same low risk as a person who never smoked.
10. **T F** Eating saturated fats contributes to high blood-cholesterol level.
11. **T F** Look for products marked "low in cholesterol" to reduce the intake of saturated fats.
12. **T F** You must exercise 20-30 minutes 6 days/week to maintain cardiovascular fitness.

13. **T** **F** "No pain, no gain" is a good rule of thumb for achieving cardiovascular fitness.
14. **T** **F** High blood pressure does not have specific, easy-to-recognize signals.

ANSWERS TO ACTIVITIES

FILL-IN-THE-BLANKS

1. Pain or pressure in the chest that does not go away, or goes away and comes back
2. Breathing difficulty, changes in pulse rate (faster or slower than normal or irregular) and unusual skin appearance
3. Five key risk factors associated with an increased incidence of cardiovascular disease:
   - Smoking
   - A high-fat diet
   - High blood pressure
   - Being overweight
   - Exercising too little

MULTIPLE CHOICE

1. **b and c are both correct** (First call EMS personnel. Then help the person rest comfortably, assist with any prescribed medication, and try to find out medical information about the person.)
2. **d is correct** (People delay getting medical care for chest pain for a number of reasons, including that they confuse possible heart attack signals with muscle soreness, they believe they have indigestion and they and other people fail to recognize the key signals of heart attack.)
3. **d is correct** (Call EMS personnel at once if chest pain or discomfort does not go away within 3 to 5 minutes or goes away and comes back.)
4. **c is correct** (Although a, b, and d are elements of care for a heart attack, the first thing you should do if you suspect a person is having a heart attack is to have the person stop whatever he or she is doing and rest. Then send someone to call EMS personnel or make the call yourself.)
5. **a, b, c, d are all correct** (A regular exercise program has many benefits, such as maintaining a healthy heart.)
6. **b is correct** (Weight-control programs are often necessary for people—young and old; in addition, weight-control programs commonly include dietary change and seldom allow you to eat whatever you want.)

TRUE/FALSE

1. F (Cardiac arrest, a condition where the heart completely stops functioning altogether or functions too poorly to circulate blood can result from a heart attack. A heart attack occurs when the heart does not receive enough blood and oxygen to function properly, which may include beating irregularly.)
2. T (Persistent chest pain or pressure that lasts more than a few minutes or goes away and comes back can signal a heart attack.)
3. F (The sitting position often makes it easier for a person having a heart attack to breathe.)
4. T (Other causes include drowning, choking, drugs, severe brain injury and severe electric shock.)
5. F (It is never too late to begin a healthy lifestyle. Making lifestyle changes, such as reducing dietary fat, increasing exercise, losing weight and stopping smoking, at any age can slow the progress of heart disease and thus help reduce the risk of heart attack.)
6. T (The risk of having a heart attack is much greater when one risk factor, such as smoking, is combined with another, such as a diet high in fat.)
7. T (Although a heart attack might come by surprise, the heart disease that causes the heart attack develops over a number of years.)
8. F (Behaviors that can have a detrimental impact on the heart—such as smoking and subsisting on junk food—can begin in childhood.)
9. T (Quitting smoking rapidly reduces the risk of heart disease.)
10. T (Saturated fats raise blood cholesterol by interfering with the body's ability to remove cholesterol from the blood. Beef, lamb, veal, pork, ham, whole milk and whole-milk products are high in saturated fats.)
11. F (Products low in cholesterol actually may be high in saturated fats.)
12. F (Researchers believe that exercising properly for 20–30 minutes at least 3 days each week is the minimum level of exercise for cardiovascular fitness.)
13. F (Feeling pain often means you are exercising improperly.)
14. T (Frequent health checkups are important to detect high blood pressure.)

6

LESSON

CPR AND UNCONSCIOUS CHOKING—ADULT AND CHILD

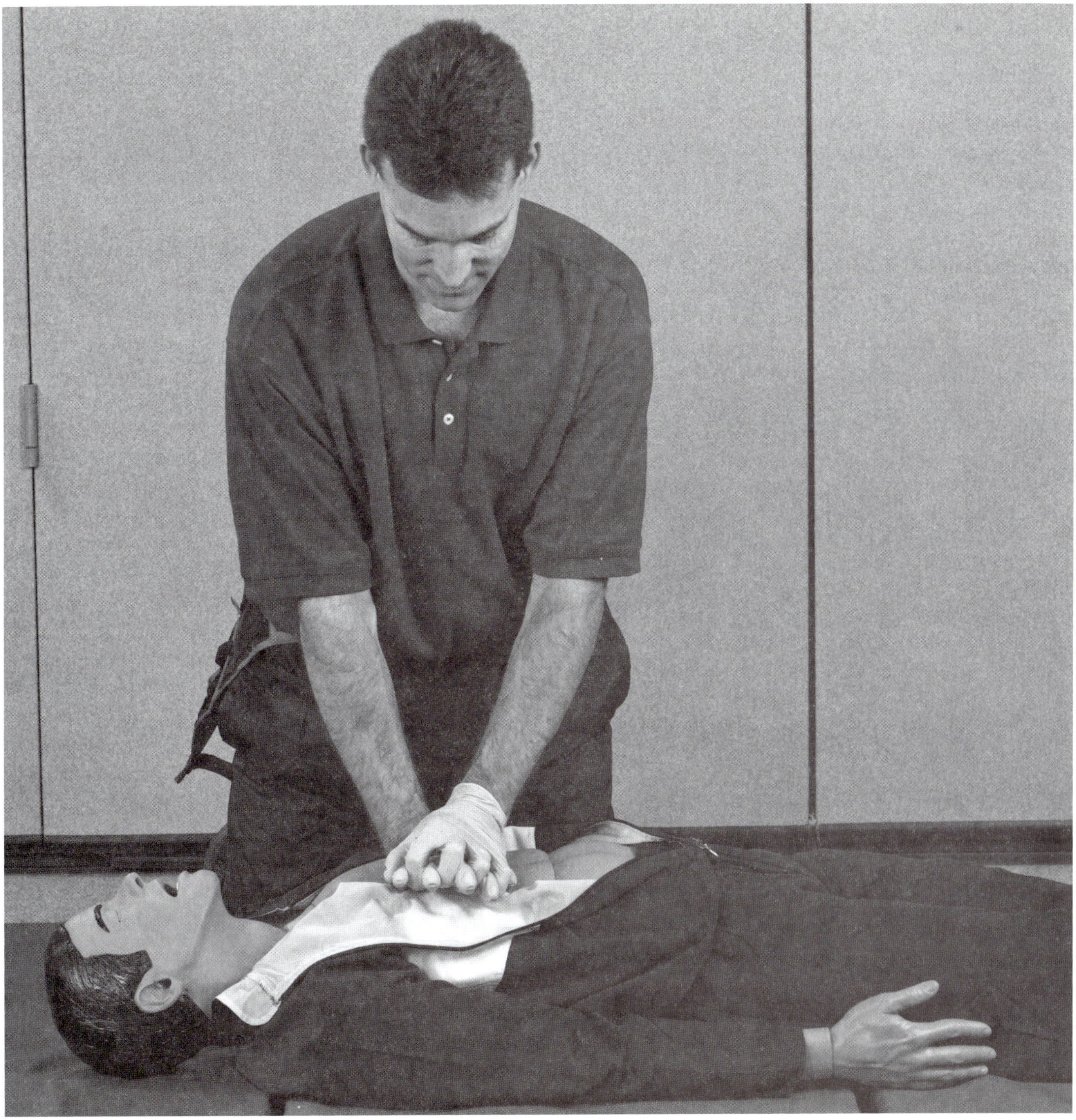

6 LESSON

CPR AND UNCONSCIOUS CHOKING—ADULT AND CHILD

ADULT CPR

An adult (ages 9 and older) is in cardiac arrest if he or she is unconscious and shows no signs of circulation (normal breathing, coughing or movement in response to rescue breaths or a pulse). *Loss of these signs of circulation can signal a cardiac arrest.*

A rescuer can help circulate blood containing oxygen by compressing the person's chest and giving rescue breaths—a procedure called cardiopulmonary resuscitation or CPR.

CPR is important for survival. For a victim of cardiac arrest to survive, the following must occur:

1. Early recognition and access to the EMS system
2. Early CPR
3. Early defibrillation
4. Early advanced medical care

Remember, this is known as the Cardiac Chain-of-Survival.

Giving Adult CPR

If you find an athlete who is unconscious, and show no signs of circulation—

Follow standard precautions.

- Perform chest compressions:
  - Locate the proper hand position on the breastbone.
  - Place the shoulders over the hands.
  - Compress the chest about 2 inches.
  - Lift up, but keep contact with the chest.
  - Repeat compressions, doing 15 compressions in about 10 seconds.
- Stop chest compressions and give rescue breaths.
  - Give 2 slow rescue breaths.
- Continue the 15-compressions/2-breaths cycle for about 1 minute (about 4 cycles).

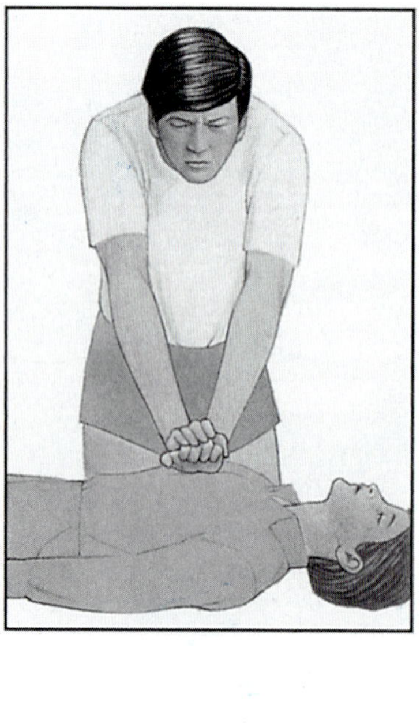

- Recheck for signs of circulation.
- If there are no signs of circulation, continue sets of 15 compressions and 2 breaths until an AED becomes readily available or EMS personnel arrive and take over. Check for signs of circulation every few minutes thereafter.

See the Sport Safety Training Handbook p. 109 for Checking an Unconscious Athlete—CPR—Adult (age 9 and older).

When to Stop CPR—

- If another trained person takes over CPR for you;
- If EMS personnel arrive and take over care of the person;
- If an AED becomes readily available;
- If you are exhausted and unable to continue;
- If the scene becomes unsafe; or
- If signs of circulation return.

SKILL PRACTICE

Use the skill sheet on the following pages to guide your practice of the skill of adult CPR.

CPR TO AN ATHLETE—ADULT

Complete "Checking an Unconscious Athlete—Adult or Child," pages 11-13.

Follow the Emergency Action Steps, CHECK, CALL, CARE. Follow standard precautions. When checking the athlete, if no signs of circulation are found, give CPR—

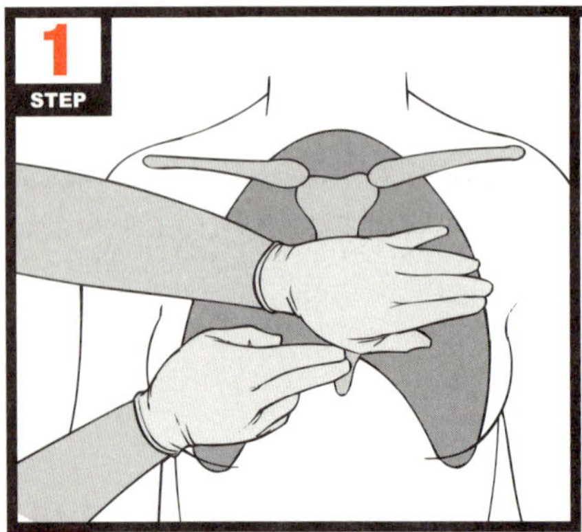

Find the hand position in the center of the chest over the breastbone.

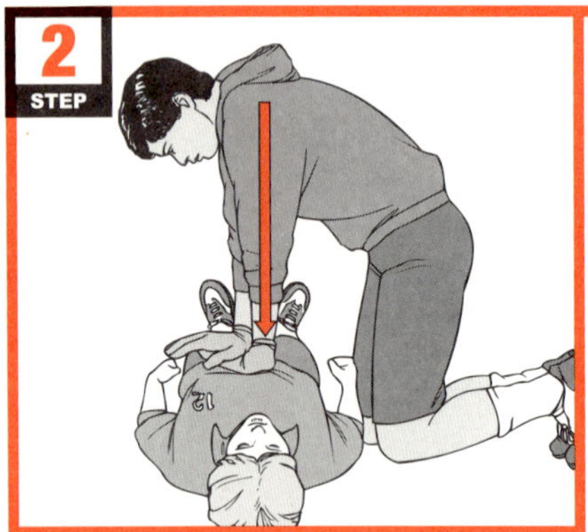

Position the shoulders over the hands. Compress the chest smoothly to a depth of about 2 inches 15 times in about 10 seconds.

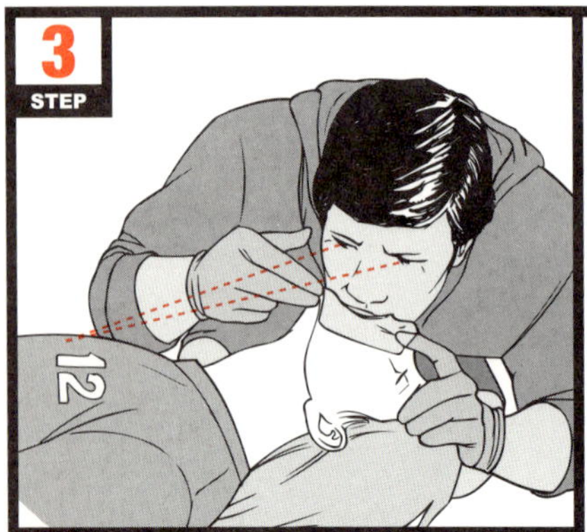

Give 2 rescue breaths.

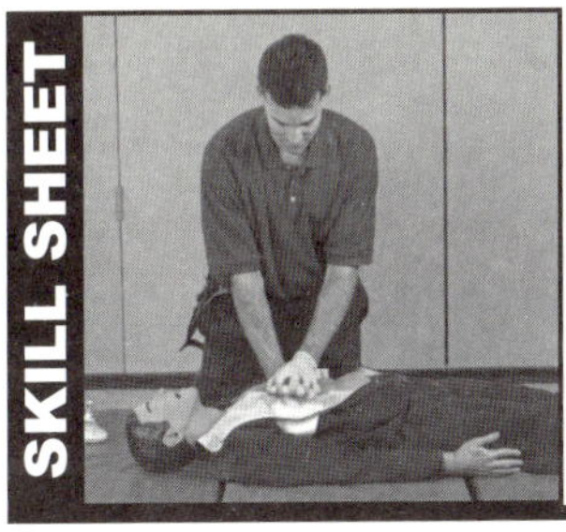

CPR TO AN ATHLETE—ADULT

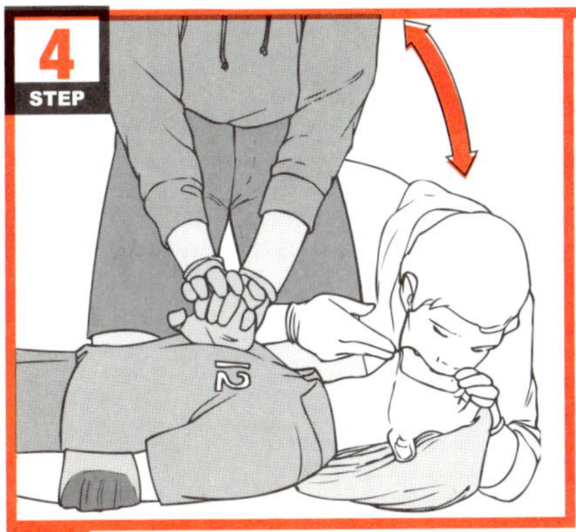

Do 3 more sets of 15 compressions and 2 rescue breaths

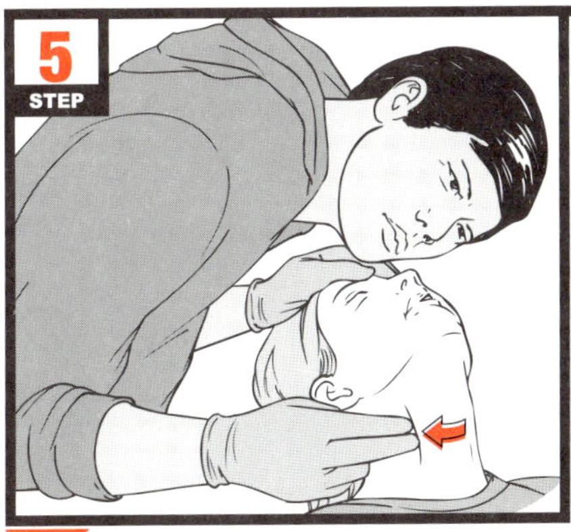

Recheck for signs of circulation for no more than 10 seconds.

If there are still no signs of circulation—

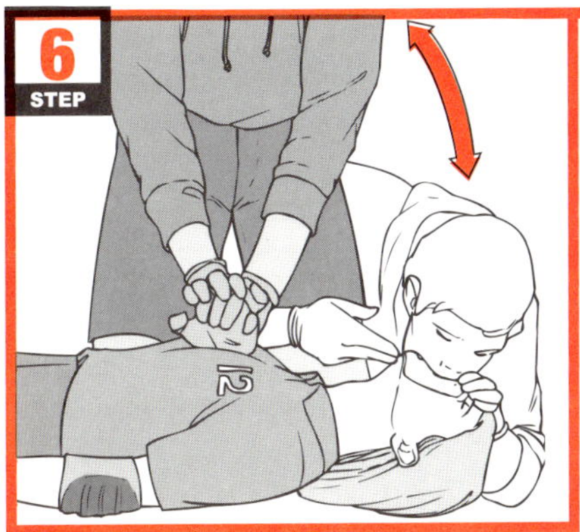

Continue sets of 15 compressions and 2 rescue breaths. Recheck for signs of circulation every few minutes.

UNCONSCIOUS CHOKING ATHLETE—ADULT

If you attempt rescue breaths but are unable to make the chest clearly rise, you must act quickly to get air into the victim. The care for an unconscious choking adult is very similar to the skill of adult CPR, with the exception that you look for a foreign object between compressions and breaths. Chest compressions are used to help force air from the person's lungs to dislodge the object.

SKILL PRACTICE

Use the skill sheets on the following pages to guide your practice of the skill of clearing an obstructed airway in an unconscious adult or child athlete.

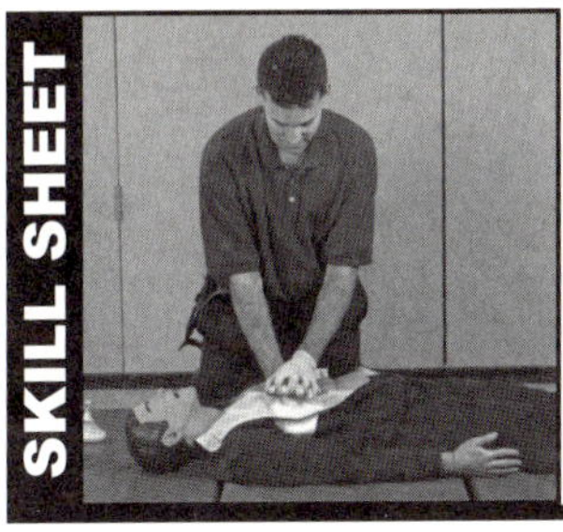

UNCONSCIOUS CHOKING ATHLETE—ADULT

Complete "Checking an Unconscious Athlete – Adult or Child," pages 11-13.

Follow the emergency action steps* CHECK, CALL, CARE*. Follow standard precautions. When checking the athlete, if breaths do not go in…

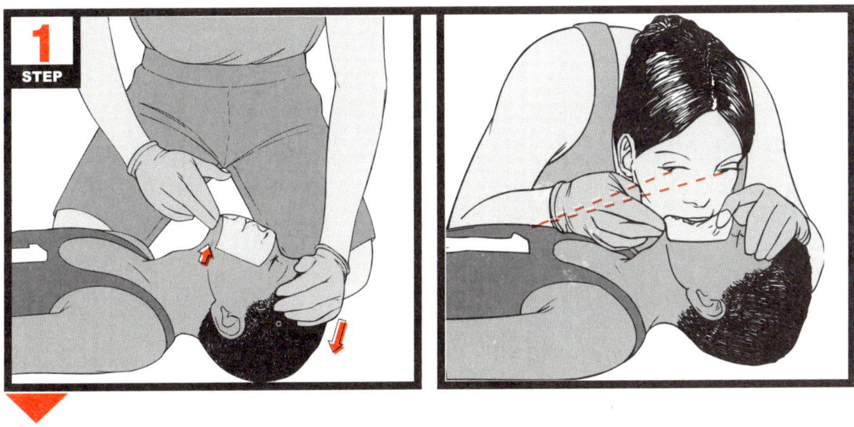

Reposition the airway by tilting the head further back and try 2 rescue breaths again.

If air (breaths) still does not go in—

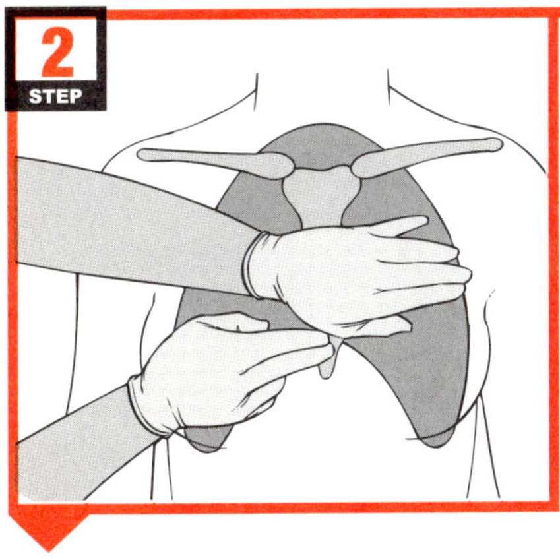

Find hand position on the breastbone.

Continued on next page.

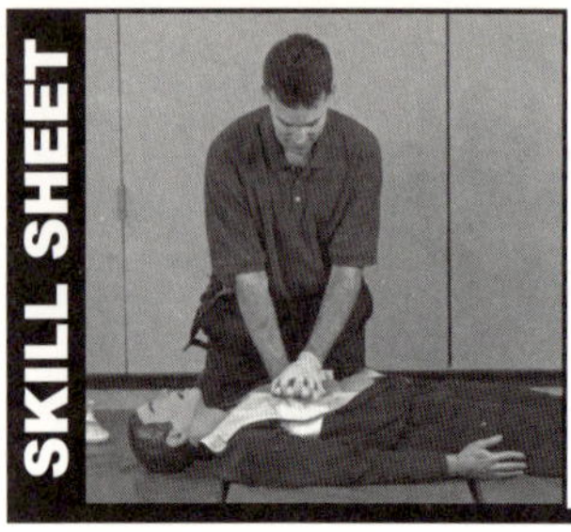

UNCONSCIOUS CHOKING ATHLETE—ADULT

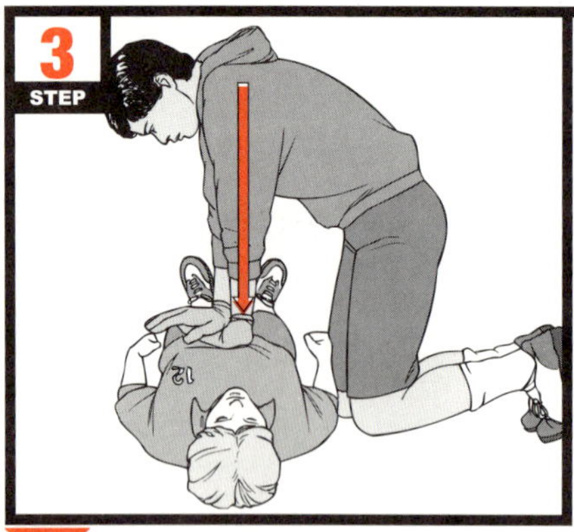

Position the shoulders over the hands.

Compress the chest 15 times to a depth about 2 inches deep.

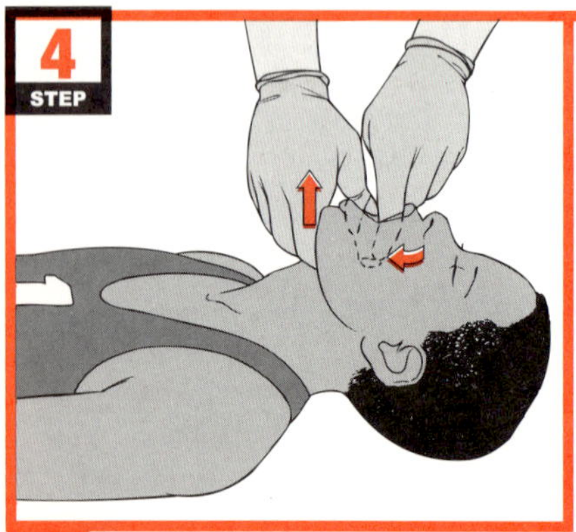

Lift the jaw and tongue and look inside the mouth.

If you see an object, remove it with a finger.

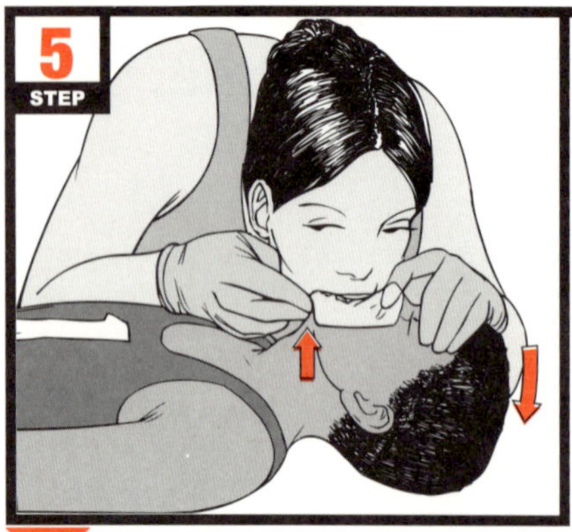

Give 2 rescue breaths.

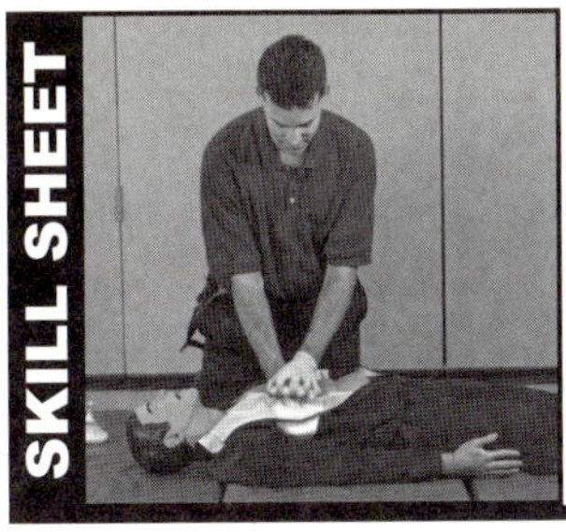

UNCONSCIOUS CHOKING ATHLETE—ADULT

If the air (breaths) still does not go in—

STEP 6

Continue steps 2-5 until—

You can breathe into the adult and make the chest clearly rise.

The person starts to breathe.

EMS personnel arrive.

If the air (breaths) goes in—

STEP 7

Check for signs of circulation (for no more than 10 seconds).

STEP 8

If the athlete shows signs of circulation but is not breathing, give rescue breathing.

OR

If the athlete shows no signs of circulation, give CPR.

CHILD CPR

A child (1 to 8 years old) is in cardiac arrest if he or she is unconscious and shows no signs of circulation (normal breathing, coughing or movement in response to rescue breaths or a pulse). *Loss of these signs of circulation can signal a cardiac arrest.*

A rescuer can help circulate blood containing oxygen by compressing the child's chest and giving rescue breaths. This is called cardiopulmonary resuscitation or "CPR."

Remember, the Cardiac Chain-of-Survival. For a victim of cardiac arrest to survive, the following must occur:

1. Early recognition and early access to the EMS system
2. Early CPR
3. Early defibrillation
4. Early advanced medical care

Most cardiac arrests in children are not sudden. The most common causes of cardiac arrest in children are:

- Airway Problems
- Breathing problems
- Trauma or an accident (e.g., automobile, drowning, electrocution or poisoning)
- A hard blow to the chest (i.e., Commotio Cordis)
- Congenital heart disease
- Sudden Infant Death Syndrome (SIDS)

Performing Child CPR

If you find a child who is unconscious and shows no signs of circulation—

Follow standard precautions.

If alone, provide 1 minute of care, then call.

- Perform chest compressions:
  - Locate the proper hand position on the breastbone:
    - Place one hand on the child's chest and the other hand on the forehead to maintain an open airway.
  - Place the shoulder over the hand.
  - Compress the chest smoothly about 1½ inches using the heel of one hand.
  - Lift up, but keep contact with the chest.
  - Repeat compressions, doing 5 compressions in about 3 seconds.

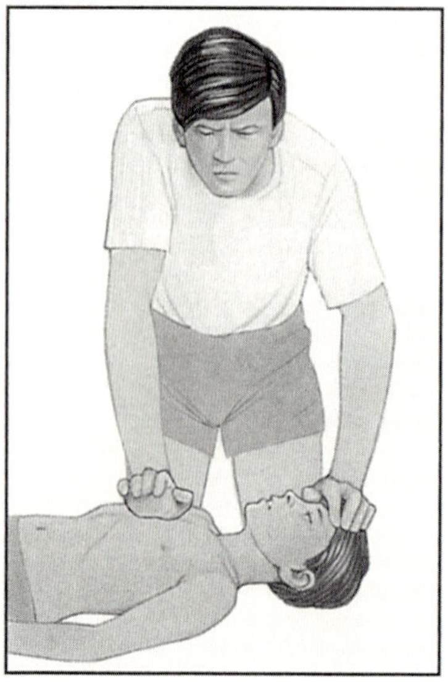

- Stop chest compressions and give rescue breath.
  - Give 1 slow rescue breath.
- Continue the 5 compressions/1 breath cycle for about 1 minute. (about 11 more cycles)
- Recheck for signs of circulation.
- If there are no signs of circulation, continue sets of 5 compressions and 1 rescue breath until EMS personnel arrive. Check for signs of circulation every few minutes thereafter.

See the Sport Safety Training Handbook p. 111 for Checking an Unconscious Athlete—CPR—Child (ages 1 to 8).

When to Stop CPR—

- If another trained person takes over CPR for you;
- If EMS personnel arrive and take over care of the person;
- If an AED becomes readily available;
- If you are exhausted and unable to continue;
- If the scene becomes unsafe; or
- If signs of circulation return.

SKILL PRACTICE

Use the skill sheet on the following pages to guide your practice of the skill of giving CPR to a child.

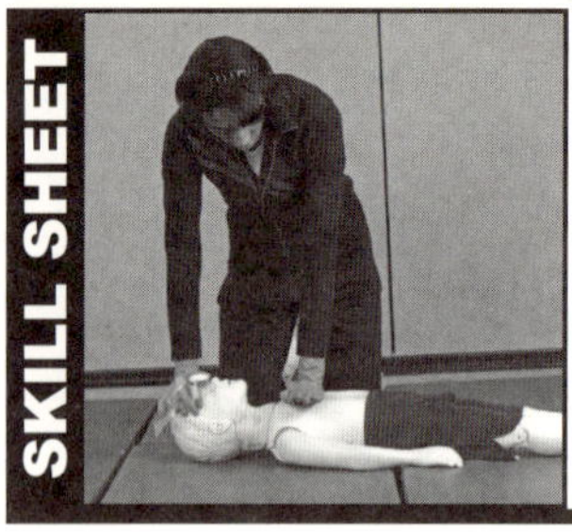

CHILD CPR

Complete "Checking an Unconscious Athlete—Adult or Child," pages 11-13.

Follow the Emergency Action Steps, CHECK, CALL, CARE. Follow standard precautions. When checking the athlete, if no signs of circulation are found, give CPR—

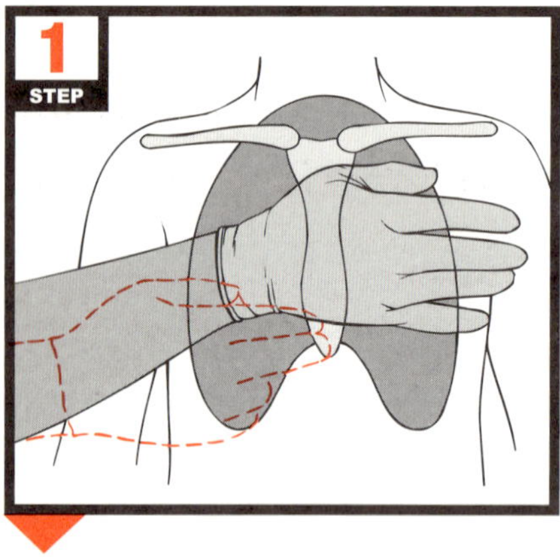

Find the hand position on about the center of the breastbone.

- **Place one hand on the child's chest and the other hand on the forehead to maintain an open airway.**

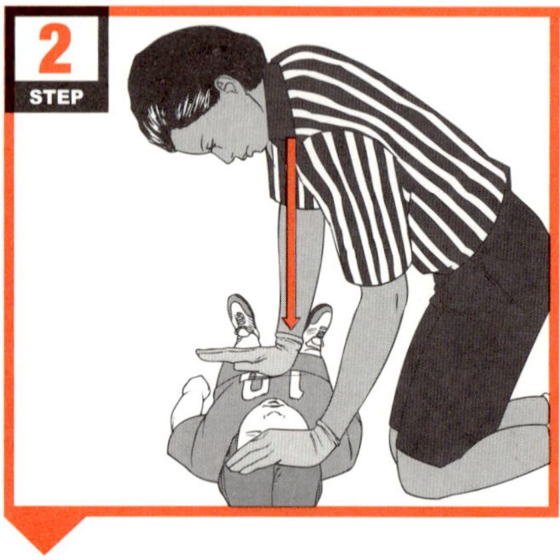

Position the shoulder over the hand.

- **Compress the chest to a depth of about $1\frac{1}{2}$ inches 5 times in about 3 seconds.**

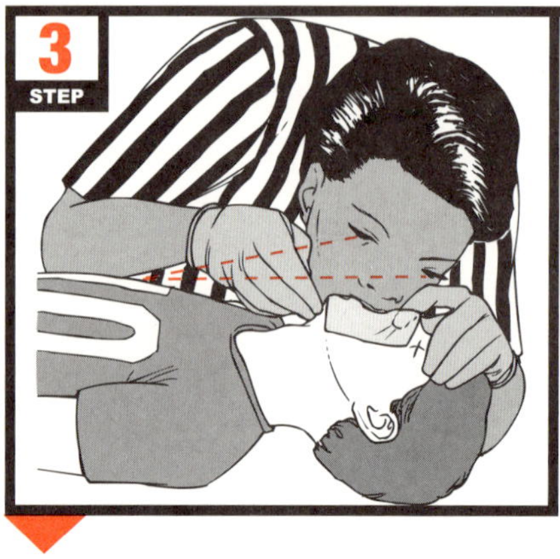

Give 1 slow breath.

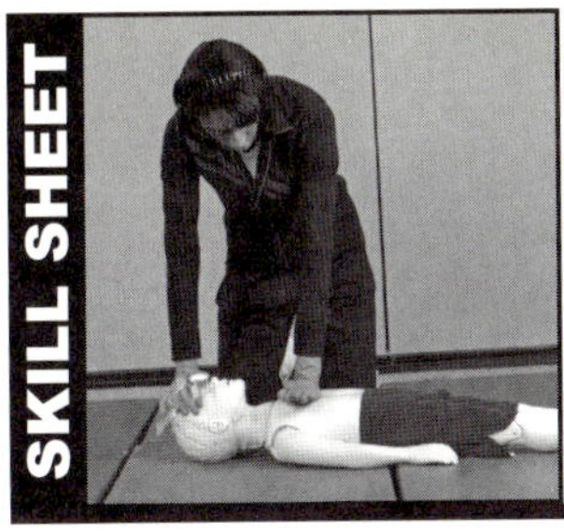

CHILD CPR

STEP 4

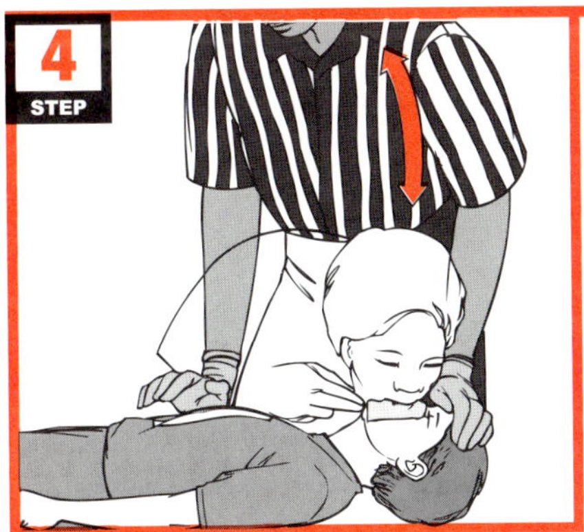

Repeat cycles of 5 compressions and 1 breath for about 1 minute.

STEP 5

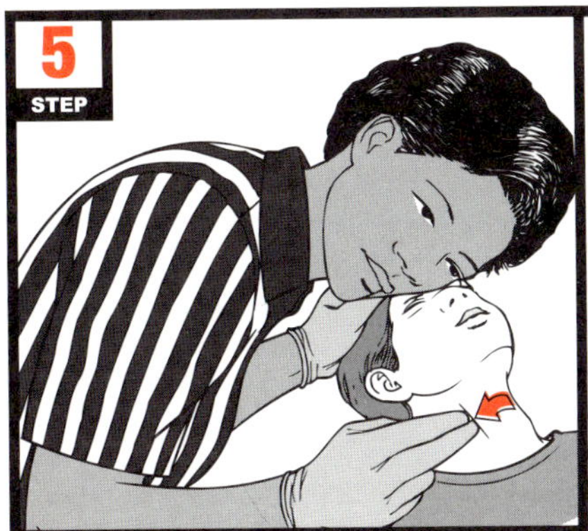

Recheck signs of circulation and breathing for no more than 10 seconds.

If there are still no signs of circulation—

STEP 6

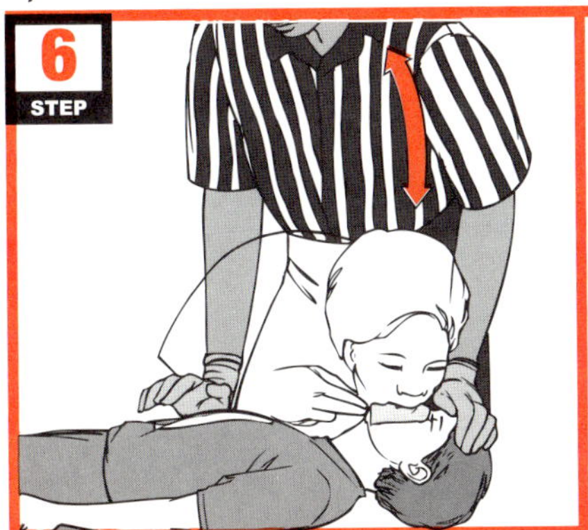

Continue sets of 5 compressions and 1 breath. Recheck signs of circulation and breathing every few minutes.

UNCONSCIOUS CHOKING ATHLETE—CHILD

The care for an unconscious choking child is very similar to the skill of child CPR, with the exception that you look for a foreign object between compressions and breaths.
Chest compressions are used to help force air from the child's lungs to dislodge the object.
If you attempt rescue breaths but are unable to make the chest clearly rise, you must act quickly to get air into the child.

Continued on next page.

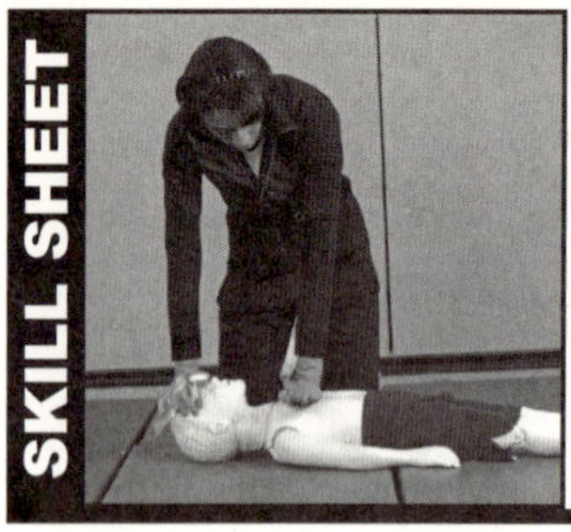

UNCONSCIOUS CHOKING ATHLETE—CHILD

Complete "Checking an Unconscious Athlete—Adult or Child," pages 11-13.

Follow the emergency action steps* CHECK, CALL, CARE*. Follow standard precautions. When checking the athlete, if breaths do not go in…

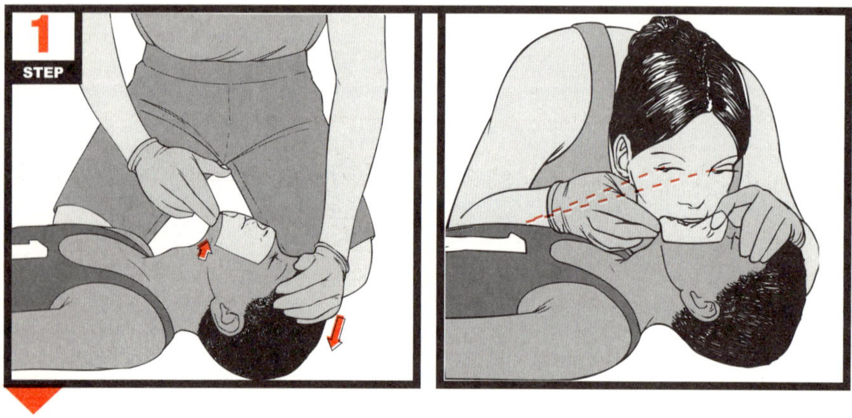

Reposition the airway by tilting the head further back and re-attempting rescue breaths.

If air (breaths) still will not go in—

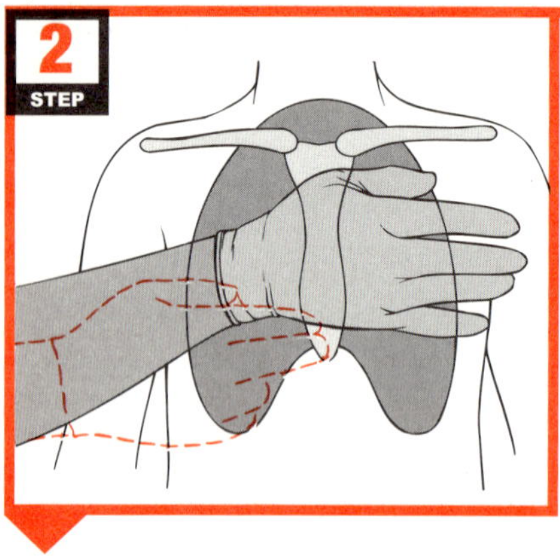

Place one hand on the child's chest and the other hand on the forehead to maintain an open airway.

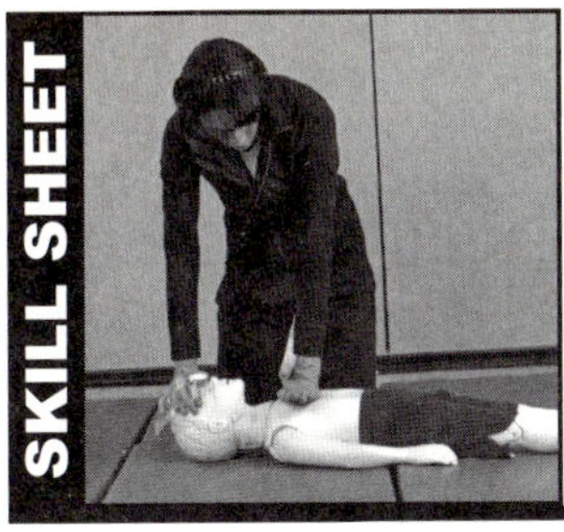

UNCONSCIOUS CHOKING ATHLETE—CHILD

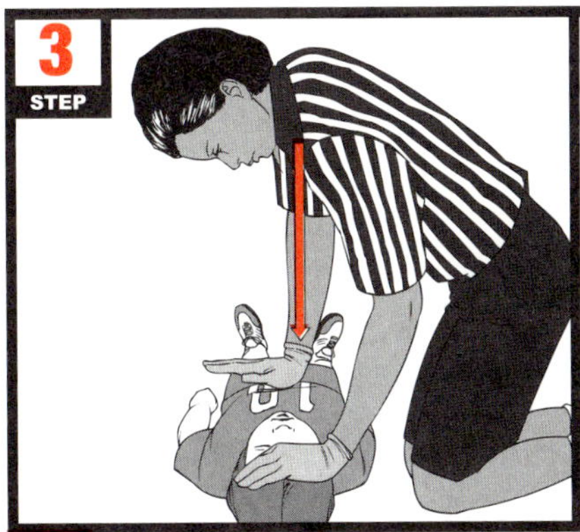

Position the shoulder over the hand. Compress the chest about 1 ½ inches deep, 5 times in about 3 seconds.

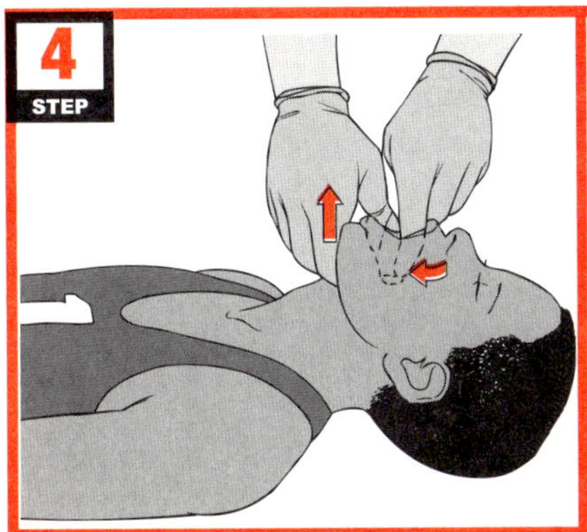

Lift the jaw and tongue and look inside the mouth. If you see an object, remove it with a finger.

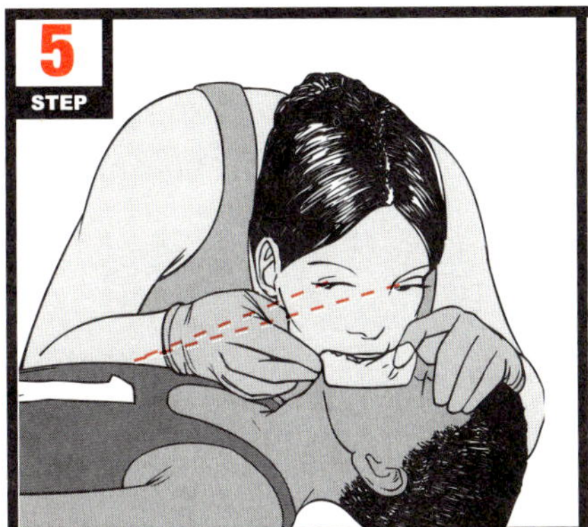

Give 1 slow breath.

Continued on next page.

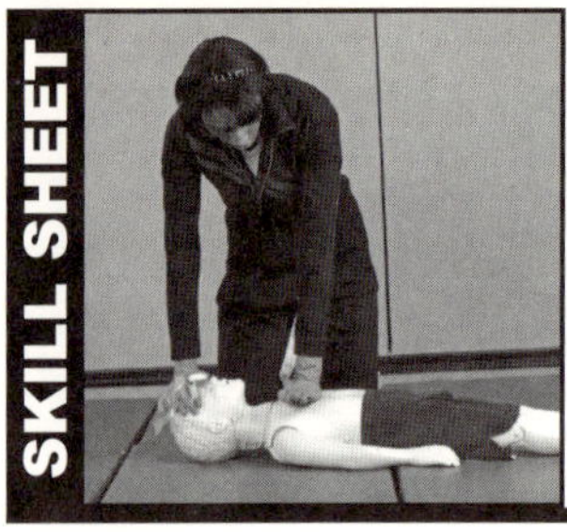

UNCONSCIOUS CHOKING ATHLETE—CHILD

If the air (breath) does not go in—

6 STEP **Repeat Steps 2–5.**

If the air (breath) does go in—

7 STEP **Give a second breath and then check for signs of circulation for no more than 10 seconds.**

8 STEP **If the child shows signs of circulation but is not breathing, give rescue breathing.**

9 STEP **If the child shows no signs of circulation, give CPR.**

ACTIVITIES

FILL-IN -THE –BLANKS

1. What are signals of cardiac arrest?

   ____

   ____

   ____

2. How does child CPR differ from adult CPR in the rate of chest compressions?

   ____

   ____

   ____

3. How does child CPR differ from adult CPR in giving rescue breaths?

   ____

   ____

   ____

4. How far do you compress a child's chest when giving chest compressions? Is this the same as for an adult's chest?

   ____

   ____

   ____

5. What are the two parts of CPR?

   ____

   ____

TRUE/FALSE

1. **T F** CPR is best performed when the person is lying on a bed or couch.
2. **T F** CPR is a combination of chest compressions and rescue breathing.
3. **T F** The signals of cardiac arrest are the same as the signals for heart attack.
4. **T F** When giving chest compressions, use your strong arm muscles to keep a steady up-and-down rhythm.
5. **T F** A person in cardiac arrest is unconscious and shows no signs of circulation.
6. **T F** Cardiac arrest is not always life threatening.

SCENARIO

Imagine yourself as the coach in the following situation. You have a first aid kit and your *Sport Safety Training Handbook*. Use your *Handbook* to answer the question for this scenario, along with information you have learned in this course.

You walk in the high school locker room before volleyball practice and find a player collapsed on the floor. A partially eaten apple is on the bench next to him. The scene is safe and you determine that the athlete is unresponsive. You call 9-1-1 or the local emergency number. What should you do next?

____

____

ANSWERS TO ACTIVITIES

FILL-IN -THE –BLANKS

1. Absence of signs of circulation
2. Child: 5 chest compressions in about 3 seconds/ Adult: 15 chest compressions in about 10 seconds
3. Child: 1 slow breath after each series of 5 chest compressions/Adult: 2 rescue breaths after each series of 15 chest compressions
4. About $1\frac{1}{2}$ inches. No, an adult's chest should be compressed about 2 inches.
5. Chest compressions and rescue breaths

TRUE/FALSE

1. F (For the greatest effectiveness, the person should be on a firm, level surface. If a person is on a bed or couch, move him or her to the floor.)
2. T (Given together, the chest compressions and rescue breathing take over for the heart and lungs. However, CPR alone is not sufficient to survive cardiac arrest. Early defibrillation with an AED and early advanced medical care must follow CPR quickly.)
3. F (Cardiac arrest often happens suddenly, without the common heart attack signals.)
4. F (Push with the weight of your upper body, not your arm muscles.)
5. T (The absence of signs of circulation is the primary sign.)
6. F (Cardiac arrest is always life threatening; the heart of a person in cardiac arrest is not circulating blood to the brain, which can cause brain cells to begin to die in a few minutes.)

SCENARIO

High School Volleyball Team

- Do not assume your player is choking.
- Open the airway and check for breathing.
- If you determine that he is not breathing, attempt 2 rescue breaths.
- If the chest does not clearly rise, reposition the airway by tilting the head further back and reattempt breaths.
- If the chest still does not clearly rise, assume the airway is blocked and perform the modified CPR technique as follows:
  - 15 chest compressions
  - Foreign object check/removal
  - Attempt 2 rescue breaths
- Repeat this cycle until the chest clearly rises, the athlete starts breathing on his own or EMS personnel arrive and take over.

7
LESSON

ADULT AED (AUTOMATED EXTERNAL DEFIBRILLATION)

7 LESSON ADULT AED (AUTOMATED EXTERNAL DEFIBILLATION)

Each year approximately 250,000 people die of sudden cardiac arrest in the United States. Sudden cardiac arrest in adults is commonly caused by an abnormal heart rhythm called ventricular fibrillation (VF). An automated external defibrillator (AED) is a machine that analyzes the heart's rhythm and, if necessary, tells you to deliver a shock to a victim of sudden cardiac arrest.

This shock, called defibrillation, may help the heart to re-establish an effective rhythm.

If the AED tells you "No shock advised," check the athlete for signs of circulation (normal breathing, coughing, or movement in response to rescue breaths, or a pulse). You may have to perform CPR. CPR begun immediately and continued until defibrillation is available helps to circulate blood that contains oxygen to the brain and vital organs. CPR is performed in conjunction with the use of an AED.

Continue CPR *until*—

- The athlete shows signs of circulation;
- The AED is ready to use;
- Another trained rescuer arrives and takes over;
- You are too exhausted to continue; or
- The scene becomes unsafe.
- When using an AED, follow these precautions:
  - Do not touch the victim while the AED is analyzing. Touching or moving the victim may affect the analysis.
  - Do not touch the victim while defibrillating. You or others could be shocked.
  - Do not use alcohol to wipe the victim's chest dry. Alcohol is flammable.
  - Do not defibrillate someone around flammable materials, such as gasoline or free-flowing oxygen.
  - Do not use an AED in a moving vehicle. Movement may affect the analysis.
  - Do not use an AED on a victim in contact with water. Move victim away from puddles of water or swimming pools or out of the rain before defibrillating.
  - Do not use an AED and/or electrode pads designed for adult victims on an infant or child under age 8 or less than 55 pounds; local protocols may differ on this and should be followed.
  - Do not use an AED on a victim wearing a nitroglycerin patch or other patch on the chest. With a gloved hand, remove any patches from the chest before attaching the device.
  - Do not use a cellular phone or radio within 6 feet of the AED. This may interrupt analysis.

SKILL PRACTICE

Use the skill sheet on the following pages to guide your practice of the skill of using an AED on an adult athlete.

USING AN AED—ADULT (AGE 9 AND OLDER)

Complete "Checking an Unconscious Athlete—Adult or Child," pages 11-13.

Follow the emergency action steps **CHECK, CALL, CARE**. *Follow standard precautions. To use an AED on an adult athlete—*

1 STEP

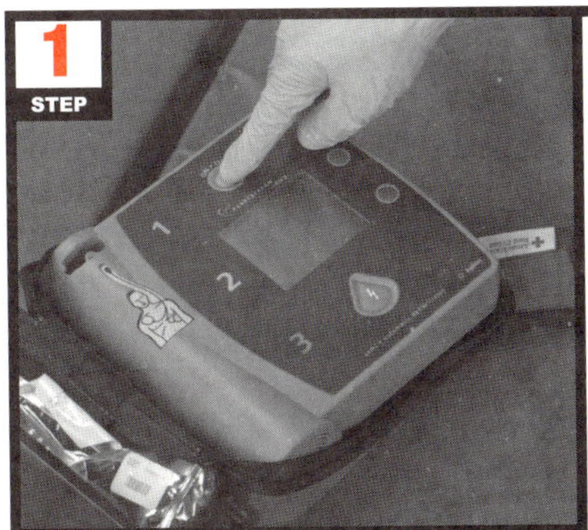

If the athlete shows no signs of circulation, turn on the AED and prepare it for use

2 STEP

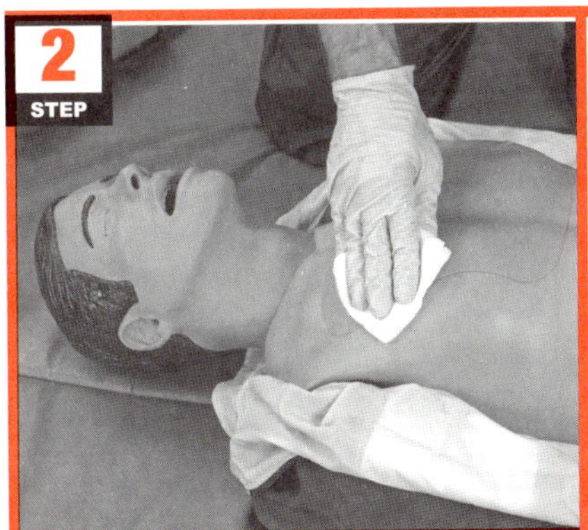

Wipe the athlete's chest dry.

Continued on next page.

USING AN AED—ADULT (AGE 9 AND OLDER)

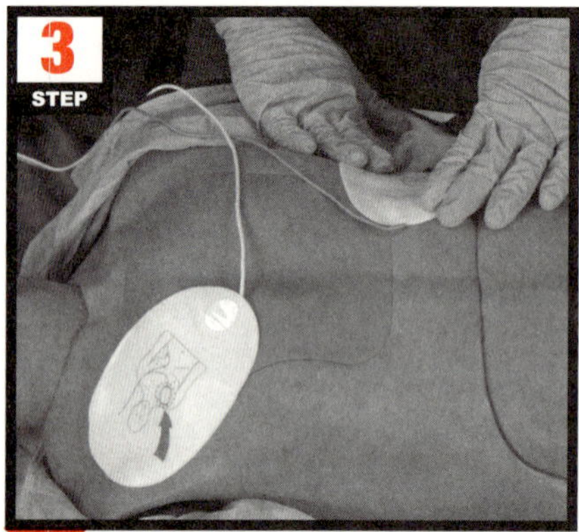

Attach the AED pads to the athlete.

- Peel one pad at a time off the backing and, following the diagram, press the pad firmly to the athlete's bare skin.
- Place one pad on the athlete's upper right chest and other pad on the lower left side.

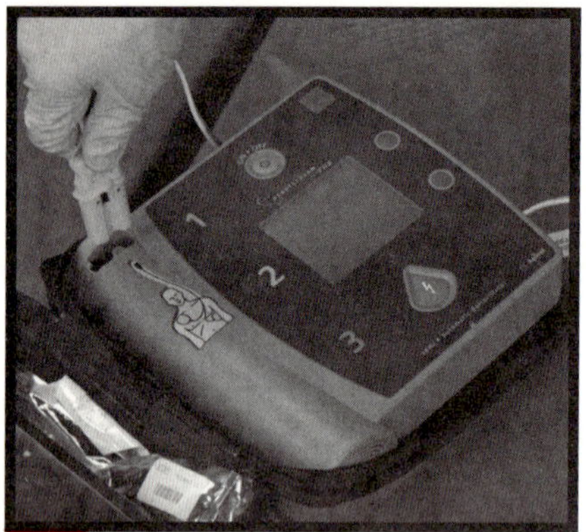

- Plug in connector, if necessary.

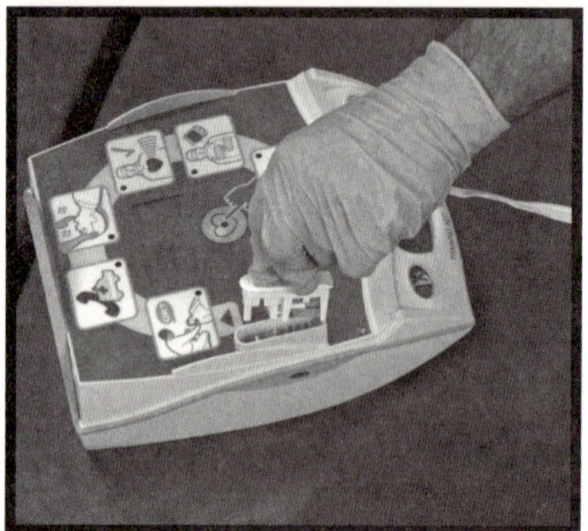

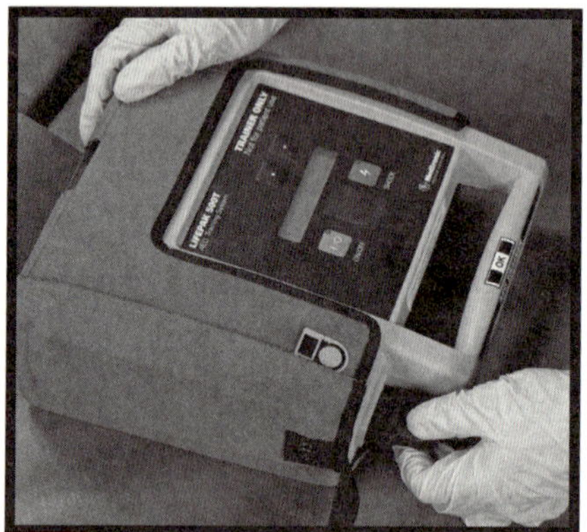

SKILL SHEET

USING AN AED—ADULT (AGE 9 AND OLDER)

4 STEP Make sure no one is touching the athlete.

- Say, "EVERYONE, STAND CLEAR!"

5 STEP Allow the AED to analyze the heart's rhythm.

6 STEP

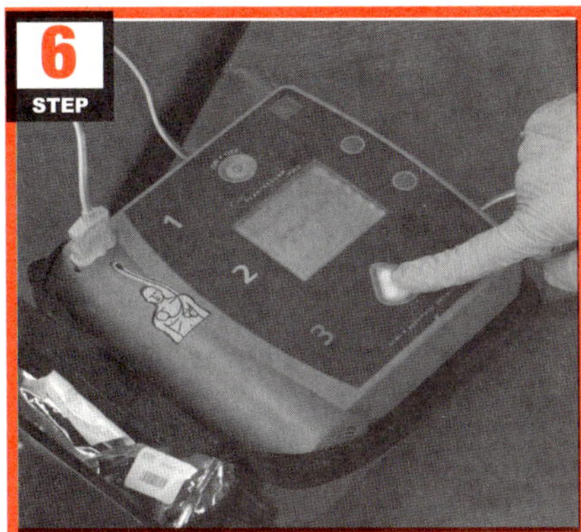

- Say, "EVERYONE, STAND CLEAR!"

Deliver a shock if prompted by pushing the "shock" button.

7 STEP Allow the AED to reanalyze.

Re-check for signs of circulation, provide additional shocks or perform CPR as necessary.

SKILL PRACTICE

Use the skill sheet on the following pages to guide your practice of the skill of using an AED on an adult athlete.

USING AN AED—ADULT CPR IN PROGRESS

Complete "Checking an Unconscious Athlete—Adult or Child," pages 11-13.

Follow the emergency action steps **CHECK, CALL, CARE**. *Follow standard precautions. When there are no signs of circulation and an AED is on the way give CPR until the AED is ready to use—*

STEP 1

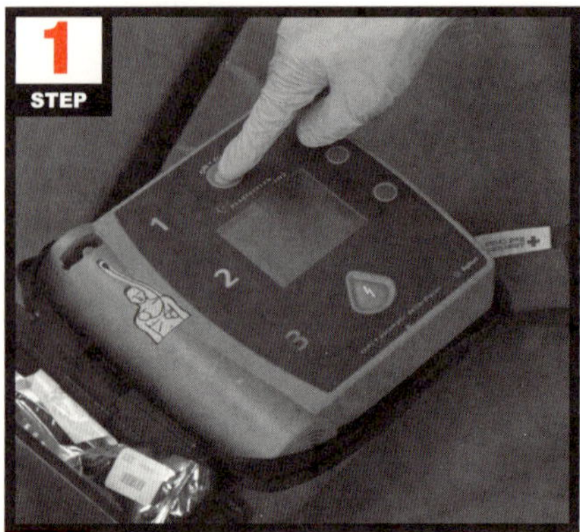

When the AED arrives, recheck for signs of circulation, if not present, turn on the AED and prepare it for use.

STEP 2

Wipe the athlete's chest dry.

STEP 3

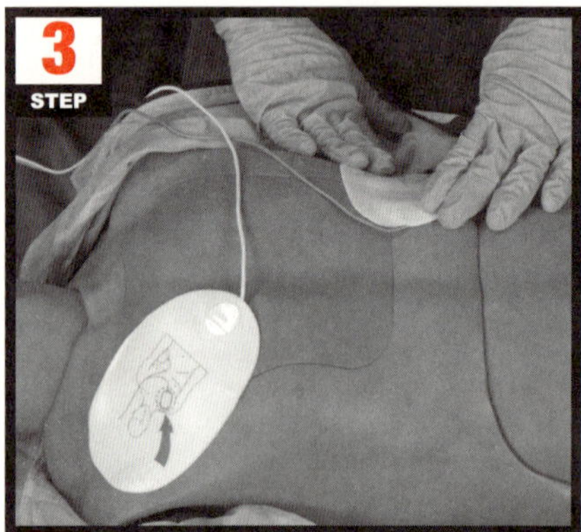

Attach the AED pads to the athlete.

- **Peel one pad at a time off the backing and, following the diagram, press the pad firmly to the athlete bare skin.**
- **Place one pad on the athlete's upper right chest and other pad on the lower left side.**
- **Plug in connector, if necessary.**

SKILL SHEET

USING AN AED—ADULT CPR IN PROGRESS

4 STEP

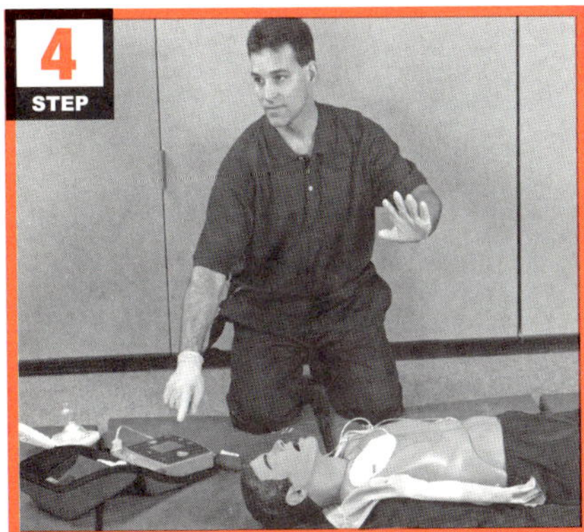

Make sure no one is touching the athlete.

- Say, "EVERYONE, STAND CLEAR!"

5 STEP

Allow the AED to analyze the heart's rhythm.

6 STEP

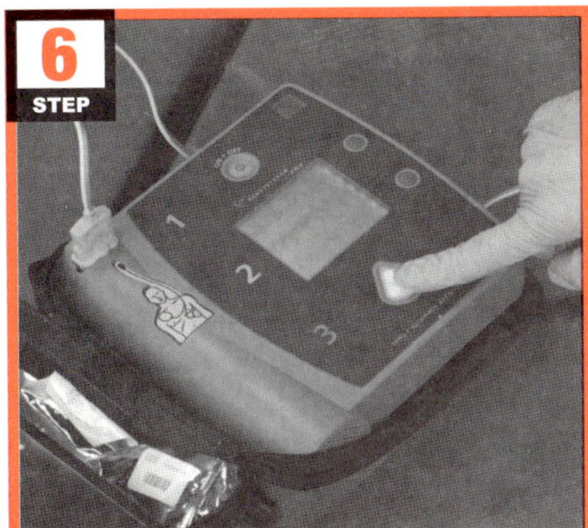

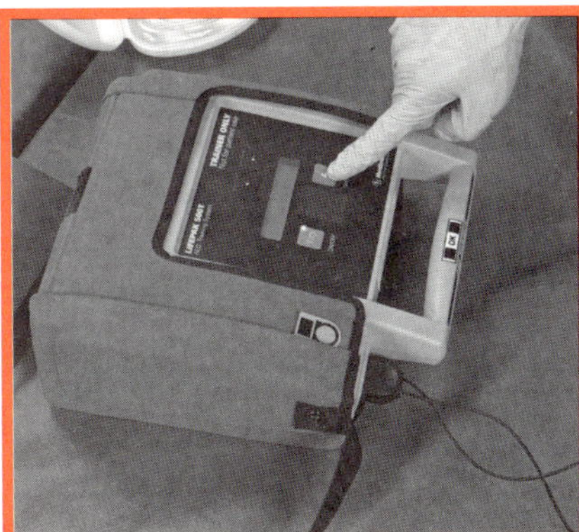

- Say, "EVERYONE, STAND CLEAR!"

Deliver a shock if prompted by pushing the "shock" button.

7 STEP

Allow the AED to reanalyze.

Re-check for signs of circulation, provide additional shocks or perform CPR as necessary.

ACTIVITIES

MULTIPLE CHOICE

Circle the answer or answers that correctly complete the following statements.

1. The purpose of CPR is to:
   a. Restart the heart
   b. Help prevent heart attacks
   c. Circulate blood containing oxygen to the vital organs
2. Should you know how to perform CPR even if you are trained to use an AED?
   a. Yes
   b. No
3. The purpose of defibrillation is to:
   a. Restore brain wave activity
   b. Establish an effective heart rhythm
   c. Control bleeding
   d. Provide oxygen to the athlete
4. If you have an AED on site, is it really necessary to call 9-1-1?
   a. Yes
   b. No

STEPS OF CARE—AED: ADULT ATHLETE

Put the following steps in correct order for using an AED on an adult. Write 1 in front of the first step to perform, 2 in front of the second, etc.

____ Stand clear-let AED analyze rhythm.
____ Stand clear-deliver a shock.
____ Place pads on athlete's bare chest.
____ Turn on the AED.
____ Plug in connector to AED if necessary.

TRUE/FALSE:

1. **T** **F** If a victim's circulation is restored, you should turn the AED off and remove the pads.
2. **T** **F** Pediatric pads should be used on an adult victim.

ANSWERS TO ACTIVITIES

MULTIPLE CHOICE

1. **c is correct:** CPR begun immediately and continued until defibrillation is available, helps to circulate blood and oxygen to the brain and vital organs. CPR should be performed until an AED is ready to use, and may have to be performed between shocks
2. **a is correct:** Yes. You may have to perform CPR if the AED determines that no shock is advised.
3. **b is correct:** The purpose of defibrillation is to establish an effective heart rhythm.
4. **a is correct:** Remember, early advanced life support is the fourth link in the cardiac chain-of-survival. If one of those links is missing, the victim's chance of survival decreases.

STEPS OF CARE—AED: ADULT ATHLETE

Correct order:
4 analyze rhythm;
5 deliver shock;
2 apply pads;
1 turn on AED;
3 plug in connector if necessary.

TRUE/FALSE:

1. F (The AED pads should not be removed nor should the AED be turned off. It is possible that the AED will tell you that additional shocks are needed.)
2. F (Pediatric AED pads **should not** be used on adult victims as they may not deliver enough energy for defibrillation.)

8 LESSON
CHILD AED (AUTOMATED EXTERNAL DEFIBRILLATION)

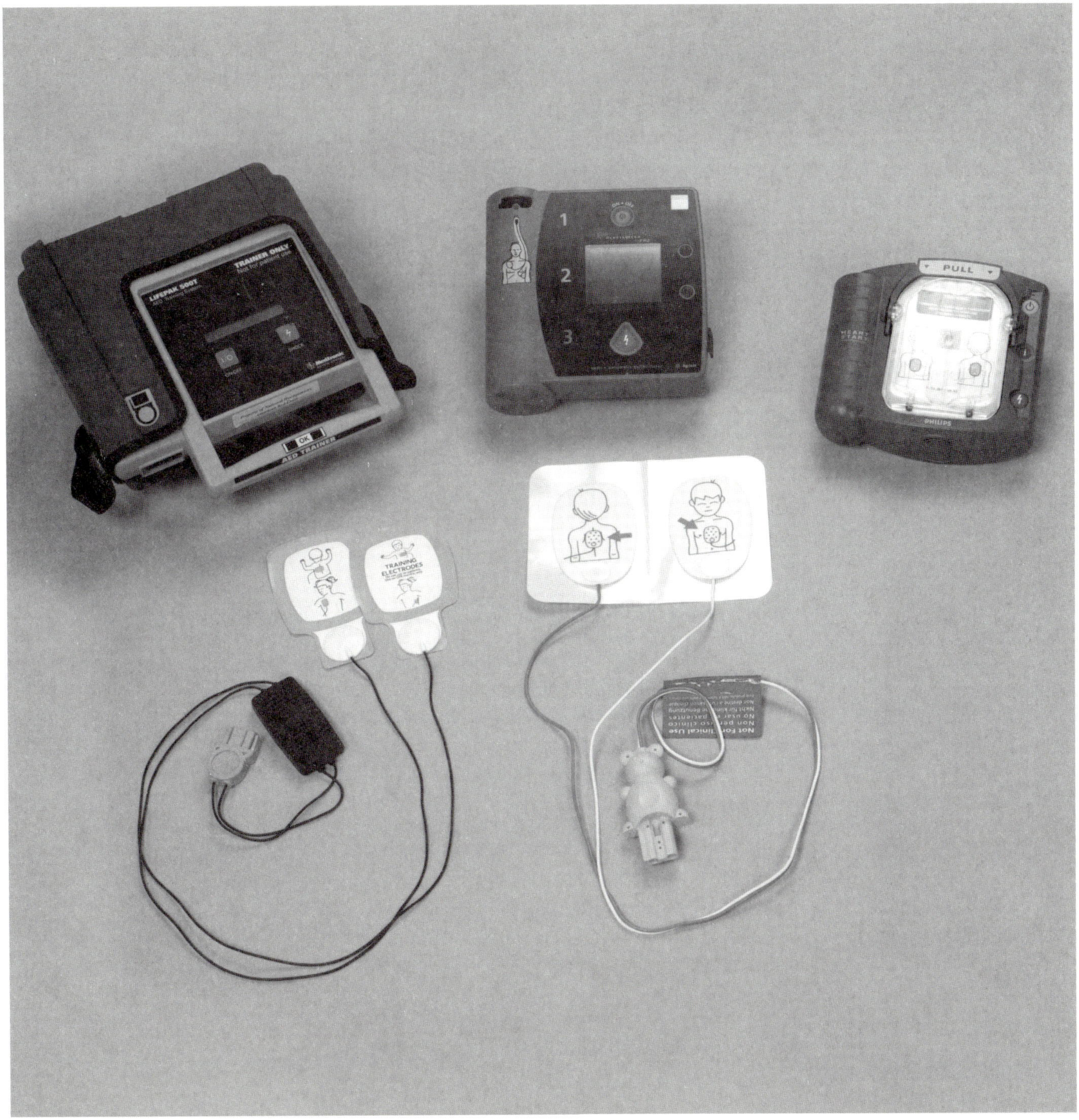

8 LESSON CHILD AED (AUTOMATED EXTERNAL DEFIBRILLATION)

Sudden cardiac arrest can happen to anyone, at any time and not just to adults. While the incidence is relatively low compared to adults, cardiac arrest resulting from ventricular fibrillation (VF) does happen to young children and infants and is no less dramatic. The emotional trauma and devastation of the loss of a child to a family and community cannot be measured.

Most cardiac arrests in children are not sudden. The most common causes of cardiac arrest in children are:

- Airway problems
- Breathing problems
- Trauma or an accident (e.g., automobile, drowning, electrocution or poisoning)
- A hard blow to the chest (i.e., Commotio Cordis)
- Congenital heart disease
- Sudden Infant Death Syndrome (SIDS)

Ventricular fibrillation is a type of an abnormal heart rhythm. This abnormal heart rhythm can occur in young children. Defibrillation is an electric shock that interrupts the heart's chaotic electrical activity and can restore the heart's ability to function as a pump. An automated external defibrillator (AED) is a machine that analyzes the heart's rhythm and, if necessary, tells you to deliver a shock to a victim of sudden cardiac arrest. Certain AEDs with pediatric AED pads are now capable of delivering lower levels of energy to a victim between the ages of 1 and 8 or less than 55 pounds. If the AED tells you "No shock advised," check the athlete for signs of circulation (normal breathing, coughing, or movement in response to rescue breaths, or a pulse). You may have to perform CPR. CPR begun immediately and continued until defibrillation is available helps to circulate blood that contains oxygen to the brain and vital organs. CPR is performed in conjunction with the use of an AED.

Continue CPR *until*—

- The child shows signs of circulation;
- The AED is ready to use;
- Another trained rescuer arrives and takes over;
- You are too exhausted to continue; or
- The scene becomes unsafe.
- When using an AED, follow these precautions:
  - Do not touch the victim while the AED is analyzing. Touching or moving the victim may affect the analysis.
  - Do not touch the victim while defibrillating. You or others could be shocked.
  - Do not use alcohol to wipe the victim's chest dry. Alcohol is flammable.
  - Do not defibrillate someone around flammable materials, such as gasoline or free-flowing oxygen.
  - Do not use an AED in a moving vehicle. Movement may affect the analysis.
  - Do not use an AED on a victim in contact with water. Move the victim away from puddles of water or swimming pools, or out of the rain before defibrillating.
  - Do not use an AED and/or electrode pads designed for adult victim on an infant or child under age 8 or less than 55 pounds; local protocols may differ on this and should be followed.
  - Do not use an AED on a victim wearing a nitroglycerin patch or other patch on the chest. With a gloved hand, remove any patches from the chest before attaching the device.
  - Do not use a cellular phone or radio within 6 feet of the AED. This may interrupt analysis.

SKILL PRACTICE

Use the skill sheet on the following pages to guide your practice of the skill of using an AED on a child athlete.

SKILL SHEET

USING AN AED—CHILD (AGE 1 TO 8 OR LESS THAN 55 POUNDS)

Complete "Checking an Unconscious Athlete—Adult or Child," pages 11-13.

Follow the emergency action steps **CHECK, CALL, CARE***. Follow standard precautions. To use an AED on a child athlete—*

STEP 1

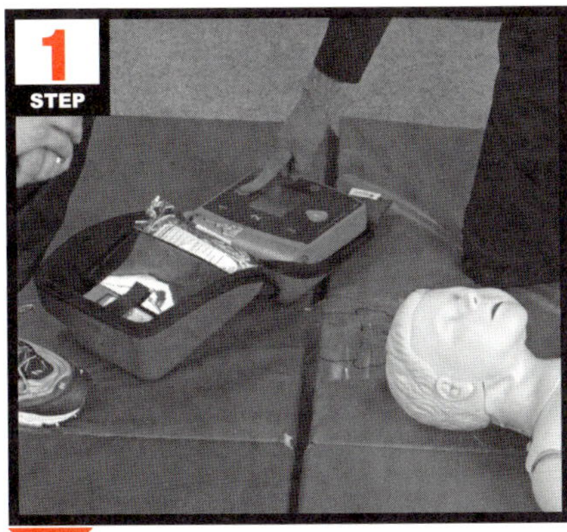

If the child shows no signs of circulation, turn on the AED and prepare it for use.

STEP 2

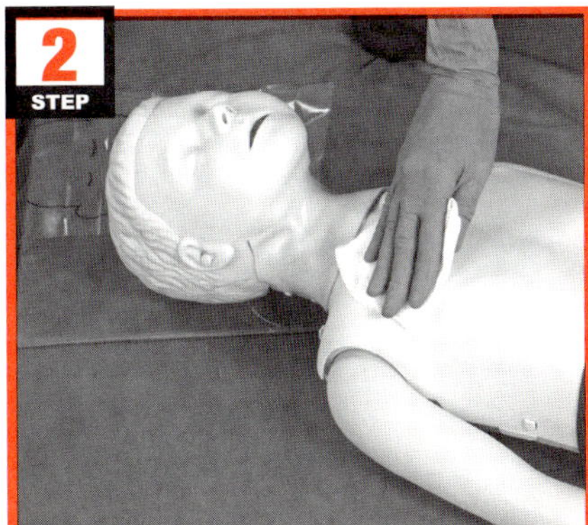

Wipe the athlete's chest dry.

Continued on next page.

SKILL SHEET

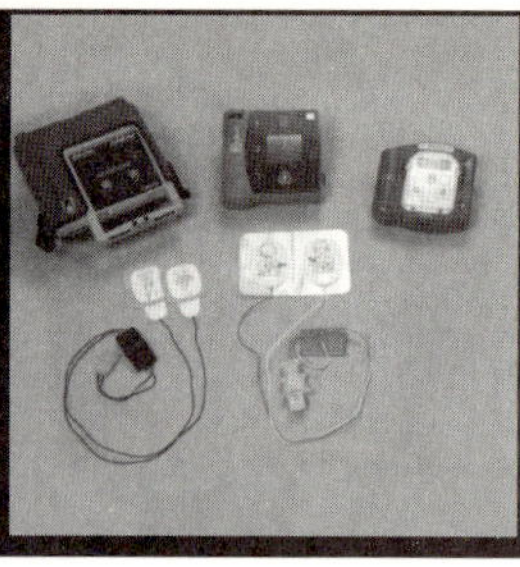

USING AN AED—CHILD (AGE 1 TO 8 OR LESS THAN 55 POUNDS)

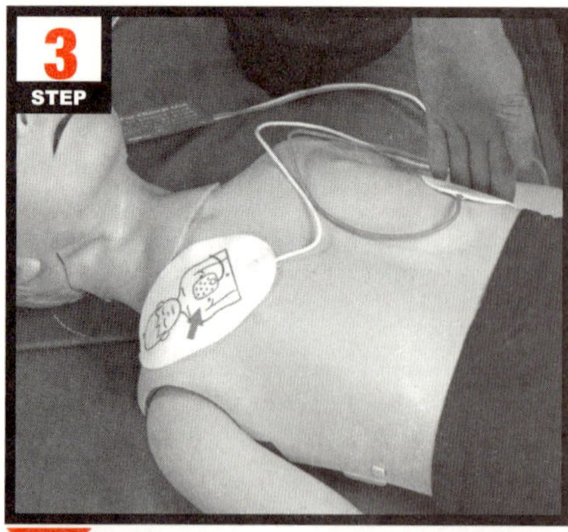

Attach the *pediatric AED pads* to the child, being certain they are *pediatric AED pads*.

- Peel one pad at a time off the backing and, following the diagram, press the pad firmly to the child's bare skin;
- Place one pad on the child's upper right chest and other pad on the child's lower left side, as long as pads do not touch each other. If they do, use front/back (anterior/posterior) pad placement instead; and

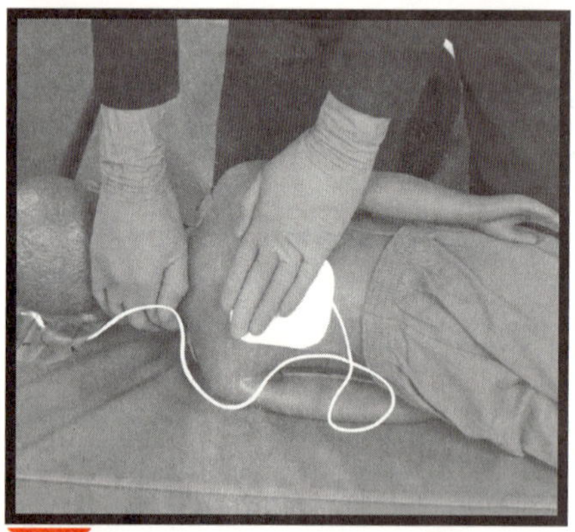

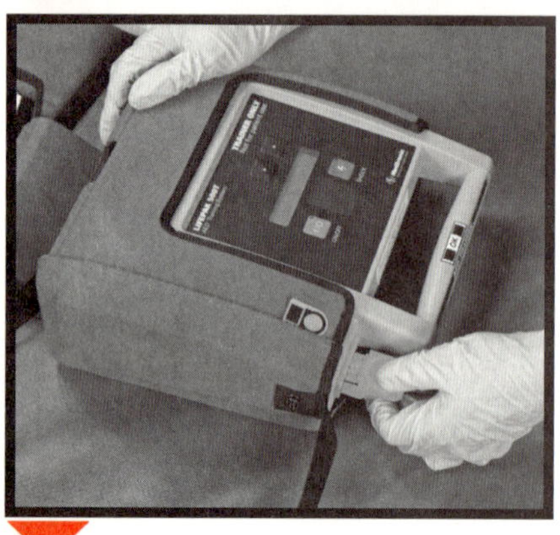

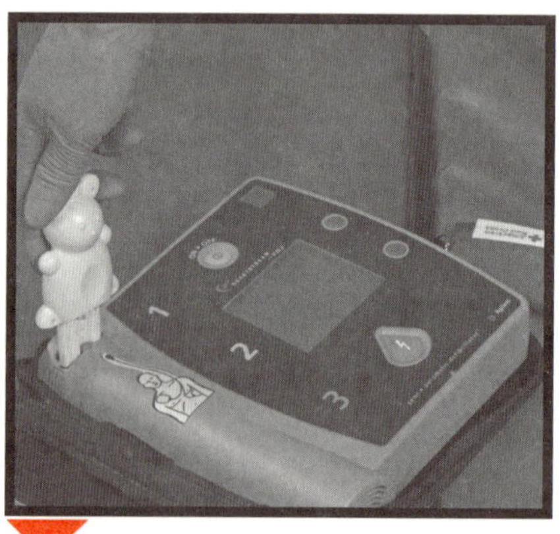

- Plug in connector, if necessary.

SKILL SHEET

USING AN AED—CHILD (AGE 1 TO 8 OR LESS THAN 55 POUNDS)

4 STEP

Make sure no one is touching the child.

- Say, "EVERYONE, STAND CLEAR!"

5 STEP

Allow the AED to analyze the heart's rhythm.

6 STEP

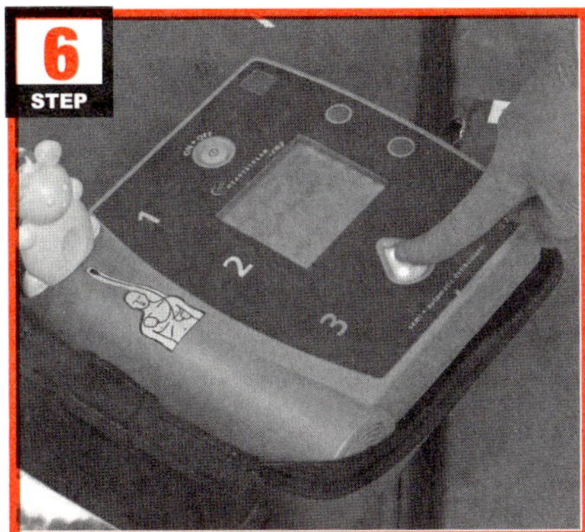

- Say, "EVERYONE, STAND CLEAR!"

Deliver a shock if prompted by pushing the "shock" button.

7 STEP

Allow the AED to reanalyze.

Re-check for signs of circulation, provide additional shocks or perform CPR as necessary.

ACTIVITIES

MULTIPLE CHOICE

Circle the answer or answers that correctly complete the following statements.

1. The purpose of CPR is to:
   a. Restart the heart
   b. Help prevent heart attacks
   c. Circulate blood containing oxygen to the vital organs
2. Should you know how to perform CPR even if you are trained to use an AED?
   a. Yes
   b. No
3. The purpose of defibrillation is to:
   a. Restore brain wave activity
   b. Establish an effective heart rhythm
   c. Control bleeding
   d. Provide oxygen to the victim
4. If you have an AED on site, is it really necessary to call 9-1-1?
   a. Yes
   b. No

STEPS OF CARE—AED: CHILD ATHLETE

Put the following steps in correct order for using a AED on a child athlete. Write 1 in front of the first step to perform, 2 in front of the second, etc.

____ Stand clear-let AED analyze rhythm.
____ Stand clear-deliver a shock.
____ Place pads on athlete's bare chest.
____ Turn on the AED.
____ Plug in connector to AED if necessary.

TRUE/FALSE

1. **T F** If a child's circulation is restored, should you turn the AED off and remove the pads?
2. **T F** Adult AED pads can be used on a child.
3. **T F** You should use the front/back (anterior/posterior) pad placement method if the pediatric pads touch each other when placed on a child's chest.

ANSWERS TO ACTIVITES

MULTIPLE CHOICE

1. **c is correct:** CPR begun immediately and continued until defibrillation is available, helps to circulate blood and oxygen to the brain and vital organs. CPR should be performed until an AED is ready to use, and may have to be performed between shocks
2. **a is correct:** Yes. You may have to perform CPR if the AED determines that no shock is advised.
3. **b is correct:** The purpose of defibrillation is to establish an effective heart rhythm.
4. **a is correct:** Remember, early advanced life support is the fourth link in the cardiac chain-of-survival. If one of those links is missing, the victim's chance of survival decreases.

STEPS OF CARE—AED: CHILD ATHLETE

Correct order:
4 analyze rhythm,
5 deliver shock;
2 apply pads;
1 turn on AED;
3 plug in connector if necessary.

TRUE/FALSE

1. F (The AED pads should not be removed nor should the AED be turned off. It is possible that the AED will tell you that additional shocks are needed.)
2. F (Adult AED pads **should not** be used on child as they may deliver too much defibrillation energy.)
3. T

9

LESSON

COACHING RESPONSIBILITIES AND SPORTS INJURY PREVENTION

9 LESSON

COACHING RESPONSIBILITIES AND SPORTS INJURY PREVENTION

SPORTS INJURIES

About half of all sports injuries can be prevented. Each season, up to 22 percent of girls and 39 percent of boys, who participate in organized sports, are injured.*

Estimated sports injuries occurring annually in the United States(injuries serious enough to require emergency room visits, 1998).

Baseball	180,582
Basketball	631,186
Bicycling/pedal cycling	577,621
Gymnastics	31,446
Soccer	169,734
Softball	132,000
Swimming	49,331
Volleyball	66,191
Weight training	60,039

GENERAL CAUSES OF SPORTS INJURIES OR ILLNESS

- Unsafe conditions, such as playing surface, equipment, weather or climate conditions.
- Unsafe actions by athletes during play, such as unnecessary roughness, breaking rules.
- Unsafe actions by athletes away from play, such as substance abuse, poor nutrition.
- Lack of proper supervision.
- Lack of appropriate physical conditioning necessary for the activity.
- Poor hygiene or infection control practices.
- Return to play before an injury is healed or rehabilitated appropriately.
- Improper techniques, such as poor blocking or tackling technique.

GENERAL PRINCIPLES TO PREVENT INJURY AND ILLNESS

- Follow sport-specific safety guidelines.
- Follow guidelines for coaching responsibilities.

COACHING RESPONSIBILITIES

- Ensuring athletes have pre-participation medical approval examination for the specific activity.
- Obtaining parental permission releases.
- Having a written Emergency Action Plan.
- Checking the facility area and playing surface before practices and competitions.
- Properly selecting and fitting sports and safety equipment, inspecting it routinely and ensuring athletes use it correctly and consistently.

*Source: Estimates for Sports Injuries 1998, National Electronic Injury Surveillance System, U.S. Consumer Product Safety Commission, National Injury Information Clearinghouse

- Warning athletes of potential risks and how to prevent injuries.
- Ensuring athletes are adequately supervised in practices and competitions.
- Ensuring athletes follow locker room rules.
- Providing rules and guidance for athletes, such as drug abuse, diet, etc.
- Providing guidelines for the parents of young athletes.
- Ensuring athletes follow personal hygiene practices.
- In case of injury, taking steps to prevent further injury.

See Part 1 of the *Sport Safety Training Handbook* for specific guidelines for these safety practices.

PREVENTING SPECIFIC INJURIES

- Always follow safety precautions to prevent head, neck and back injuries (*see Handbook, p. 17*).
- Use safe practices to prevent musculoskeletal injuries, including—
  - Warm-up and cool-down exercises.
  - Planned safe training methods.
  - Preventing overuse injuries.
  - Stretching.
  - Conditioning properly.
  - Teaching of proper techniques.
  - Using proper progressions and drills.
- Prevent injuries and illness related to the environment, including—
  - Heat-related emergencies.
  - Cold-related emergencies.
  - Weather-related emergencies, such as lightning strikes.
- Follow specific guidelines to prevent dehydration during strenuous activity (*see Handbook, p. 31*).
- Understand and act to prevent nutritional abuse and eating disorders.
- Understand allergies and act to prevent allergic reactions.
- Understand exercise-induced asthma, recognize its signals and help prevent it from being a problem for affected athletes.
- Understand substance abuse and act to prevent it.
- Understand sport-related injuries common in athletes and follow accepted guidelines to help prevent them.

See Part 1 of the *Sport Safety Training Handbook* for specific guidelines for these safety practices. See the Injury Prevention Checklist on p. 16 of the *Sport Safety Training Handbook*.

GUIDELINES FOR AFTER AN INJURY OCCURS

1. Evaluate the injury and its cause.
2. Understand and follow specific return-to-play guidelines (*see Handbook, p. 49*).
3. Know how to document and report any sports injury or illness (*see Handbook, p. 51*).

See the Incident Report Form on p. 64 of the Sport Safety Training Handbook.

4. Follow specific guidelines for how and when to transport an injured athlete (*see Handbook, p. 52*).
5. Understand the value of critical injury stress debriefing and know how to obtain it (*see Handbook, p. 53*).

See Part 1 of the *Sport Safety Training Handbook* for specific guidelines for these safety practices.

ACTIVITIES

Consult Part 1 of the *Sport Safety Training Handbook* for information as needed in the following activities.

FACILITY INSPECTION

Use the checklist provided to perform a safety inspection of the facility or field before play begins (*see Handbook p. 7*); visualize your own facility. Mentally inspect it, noting areas that present risk of injury or damage to athletes or property. Physically review equipment, playing surfaces, surrounding areas, etc., as if this is the first time you have seen them. If assistants or volunteers help in your practices and competitions, think about how you would ask them to check the facility using this checklist.

FILL-IN -THE-BLANKS

Write your answers in the blank spaces.

Having a(n) ______________________ prepared in writing helps ensure you know what to do, and who to call, if an emergency occurs

Name at least four of the six factors that can make a heat-related emergency more likely:

____

____

____

____

As a general guideline to avoid dehydration, an athlete should drink __________ cups of water before a strenuous workout or competition.

MULTIPLE CHOICE

Circle the answer or answers that correctly complete the following statements.

1. All athletes should have a medical examination—
   a. Every month.
   b. Before the first practice of the season.
   c. Before the first competition of the season.
   d. At the end of the season.
   e. Once every 2 years.
2. Which of the following statements is true?
   a. With proper diligence, all sports injuries could be prevented.
   b. About half of all sports injuries can be prevented.
   c. Few sports injuries can be prevented, although the effort should still be made.
   d. Sports injuries cannot be prevented, but the extent of injury or disability can be minimized by preventive actions.
3. Coaches are responsible for supervising their athletes—
   a. At all times from the moment they enter the facility until they leave.
   b. During competitions only.
   c. During both practices and competitions.
   d. Only as described in a written statement from the sponsoring organization.
4. Which of these groups is most susceptible to overuse injury?
   a. Young athletes who are still growing
   b. Adolescent athletes who have stopped growing
   c. Young adult athletes in competition
   d. Established athletes who have competed for years
5. Exercise-induced asthma—
   a. Means certain individuals simply cannot participate in sports.
   b. Usually goes away as the athlete becomes better conditioned.
   c. Can usually be treated effectively by a doctor.
   d. Increases the athlete's likelihood of a heart attack.
6. Athletes sometimes abuse—
   a. Steroids.
   b. Marijuana.
   c. Alcohol.
   d. Amphetamines.
   e. Cocaine.
7. Coaches should document the following types of injuries occurring in practice or competition.
   a. All injuries
   b. All injuries that result in the athlete stopping the activity
   c. All injuries in which the coach tells the athlete to seek medical care
   d. All injuries for which EMS personnel are called
8. An athlete should not return to play if—
   a. Vision is affected by an eye injury.
   b. The athlete vomits twice.
   c. The athlete seems hesitant to play.
   d. The athlete's head injury seems minor.
   e. The athlete has joint pain.

TRUE/FALSE

Circle T if the statement is true; circle F if it is false.

1. **T F** Preventing sports injuries involves using safety practices appropriate in all sports and specific actions for the specific sport.
2. **T F** Warm-up exercises are important because a heart attack is less likely when the heart rate is raised slowly.
3. **T F** No athlete in organized sports has ever died as a result of being struck by lightning.
4. **T F** The only nutritional problem likely to occur among athletes results from mistaken notions of "bulking up" before a competition.
5. **T F** It is safe for you to transport an injured athlete to the hospital yourself if an upper leg fracture is not actively bleeding through a wound in the skin.

SCENARIOS

Imagine yourself as the coach in the following situations. You have a first aid kit and your *Sport Safety Training Handbook*. Use your *Handbook* to answer the questions for these scenarios, along with information you have learned in this course.

Your softball team is practicing for a major competition only a week away. It's the hottest day of the year. It's noon, the temperature is 90 degrees F and may go higher, and from the sweat breaking out on your athletes just from trotting out onto the field you can tell the humidity is high. Conditions are not so bad that you need to cancel practice, but you want to be safe. Name three things you can do before practice begins to lessen the likelihood of any player suffering a heat-related emergency.

____

____

____

After practice begins, you should continue to be careful to prevent a heat-related emergency. Name three things you can do during the practice to lessen the likelihood of any player suffering a heat-related emergency.

____

____

____

SCENARIO FOR DISCUSSION

You are the new rowing coach and are just getting to know your athletes during preseason training. All your athletes have had a physical examination, and everyone seems to be in acceptable shape. After the first real team workout, you are walking back to the locker room with the team and notice that Jeff, new on the team this year, is being razzed by teammates for being out of shape. He does seem to be breathing harder than the others, and you remember seeing him pause a couple times during the workout to catch his breath. Nonetheless, his color is good, he's breathing easier now, and he shows no signals of being ill or injured. While the team showers, you check Jeff's medical records on file—no problems are noted. Maybe he is just out of shape.

Should you forget it for now? Should you do or say anything to Jeff?

ANSWERS TO ACTIVITIES

FILL-IN -THE-BLANKS

1. emergency action plan (*see Handbook, p. 5*)
2. hot weather, high humidity, physical exertion, barrier clothing, use of salt tablets, inadequate fluid intake (*see Handbook section on preventing heat injuries, p. 25*)
3. this answer may vary somewhat depending on the sport and circumstances; generally, drink 2 cups of water 2-3 hours before a competition, 1 cup of water an hour before, and possibly an additional ½ cup of water 15 minutes before, for a total of about 3 or more cups of water (*see Handbook section on prevention of dehydration, p. 31).*

MULTIPLE CHOICE

1. **b is correct** (It is crucial that all athletes have a complete physical examination before beginning practice for the season to prevent harm from occurring due to an otherwise unseen condition. See the *Handbook* section on the preseason physical examination, p. 2).
2. **b is correct** (Because about half of all sports injuries can be prevented, following the general safety practices included in the Sport Safety Training course along with additional sport-specific guidelines to prevent injury should significantly reduce injuries to athletes that occur in practices and competitions.)

3. **a is correct** (Generally a coach is responsible for his or her athletes during the entire time they are in the coach's care. This includes from the time athletes are dropped off to the time they are picked up by parents or guardians. A specific written statement may supplement this responsibility, but lack of such a document from the facility or organization does not reduce this responsibility. See the section on supervision in the *Handbook*, p. 12.)
4. **a is correct** (Young athletes who are still growing are most susceptible to overuse injuries because their cartilage is still developing and thus is more easily damaged and their muscles and tendons are tighter because of rapid bone growth. See the *Handbook* section on prevention of overuse injuries, p. 23.)
5. **c is correct** (Exercise-induced asthma can be treated effectively by a doctor, allowing the affected athlete to participate fully in sports; it does not usually go away by itself, and it has no relationship to a heart attack. See the section on exercise-induced asthma in the *Handbook*, p. 38.)
6. **answers a-e are all correct** (An athlete, like any other person, may abuse any drug or substance for a variety of reasons; do not automatically exclude any athlete from this possibility merely on the basis of performance or personality. See the section on substance abuse in the *Handbook*, p. 38.)
7. **a is correct** (All injuries should be documented, even if the player returns to play, because documentation of the injury and other factors involved may become important later on if the injury worsens or other problems result. See the *Handbook* section on documentation, p. 51.)
8. **answers a-e are all correct** (All of these are reasons an athlete should not return to play. It is not your responsibility to diagnose how serious an injury may be—with these signals, let a doctor decide. See the return-to-play guidelines in the *Handbook*, p. 49).

TRUE/FALSE

1. T (Following general safety principles will prevent injuries in all sports; follow additional specific guidelines for injuries common in the specific sport. Consult the sport's National Governing Body, listed in the *Handbook* on p. 57, for additional information.)
2. F (Warm-up exercises are intended primarily to prevent musculoskeletal injuries; research does not show a relationship between heart attack and how fast the heart rate increases. See guidelines for warm-up and cool-down exercises in the *Handbook*, p. 21.)
3. F (Lightning strikes are actually the number one cause of death for athletes under age 10 while participating in a sport. See guidelines for environmental safety in the *Handbook*, p. 8.)
4. F (Although it is true that mistaken ideas about "bulking up" in advance of a competition can cause problems, this is not the only nutritional problem common among athletes; eating disorders, such as bulimia and anorexia nervosa, are also common in certain age groups and can cause health problems for the athlete. See nutritional guidelines in the *Handbook*, p. 35.)
5. F (Even minor injuries of the lower extremities can be problematic in transport by untrained individuals; in this case let the EMS personnel handle transport. See guidelines for transport, p. 52 in the *Handbook*.)

SCENARIOS

Softball practice

Before practice:

1. Ensure athletes are not overdressed.
2. Ensure athletes drink enough fluids before starting practice.
3. Have athletes take it slow at first and get acclimated to the heat.

During practice:

1. Make sure athletes take frequent water breaks.
2. Observe athletes closely for any signals of heat problems.
3. Reduce practice time.

SCENARIO FOR DISCUSSION

Although you don't have any real evidence of a problem, you don't want to simply ignore Jeff's condition. You might talk with Jeff in a friendly way, to see if he's had difficulty catching his breath in other situations. He may have a condition such as exercise-induced asthma or an allergy that did not show up in his physical; these conditions can be easily treated, allowing Jeff to more fully participate in the sport. Even if your conversation with Jeff suggests that he is simply out of shape, you must watch him carefully in the next practice, checking for any worsening of the problem and considering whether you should recommend a checkup by a sports physician. In addition, review your training schedule to ensure that none of your athletes is being pushed too fast.

10 LESSON

SOFT TISSUE INJURIES

10 LESSON SOFT TISSUE INJURIES

WOUNDS

- Open wounds (cuts, scrapes, lacerations, avulsions)—bleeding outside the body
- Closed wounds (bruise, internal bleeding)—bleeding inside the body

Preventing Wounds

- Appropriate clothing and equipment should be worn in all practice sessions and competitions.
- Often the causes of wound injuries can be prevented, such as falls caused by a problem with the playing surface.
- Sport-specific safety practices can prevent wounds caused by personal contact with other athletes or due to problems with equipment, the playing surface, etc.
  See also Part 1 in the Sport Safety Training Handbook *for safety practices to prevent injury.*

TYPES OF WOUNDS

Bruise

- Bleeding under the skin caused by damage to soft tissues and blood vessels.
- The area may change from red to dark red or purple.
- A large or painful bruise may signal severe damage to deep tissues.

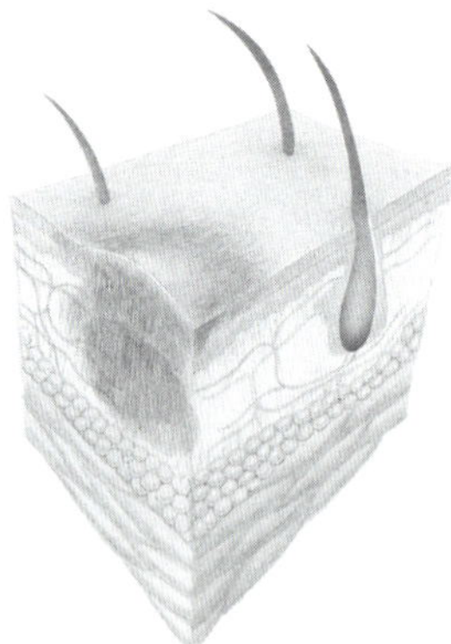

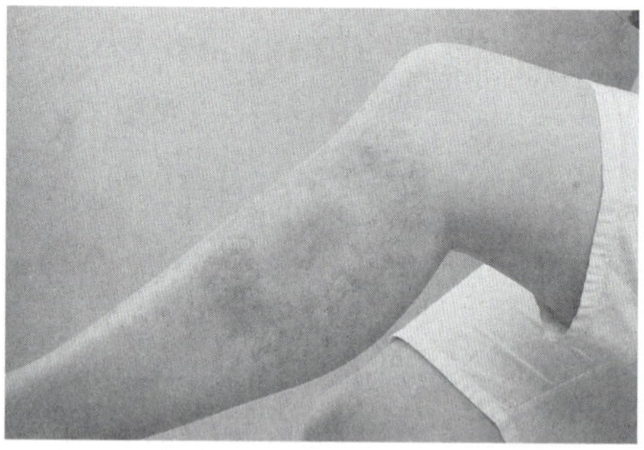

Abrasion

- Skin has been rubbed or scraped away; the area is usually painful.
- Dirt and other matter can enter the wound; cleaning the wound is important to prevent infection.

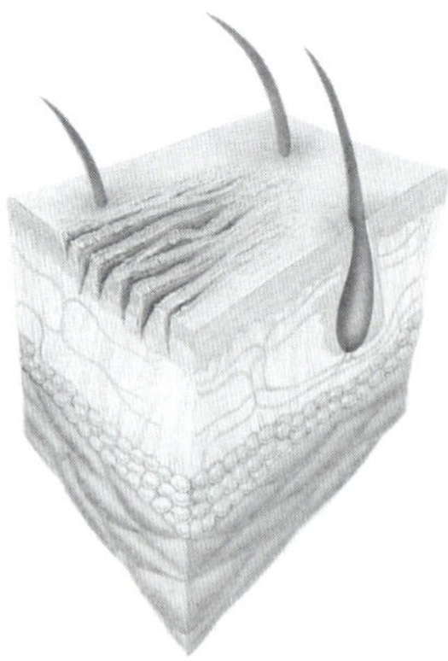

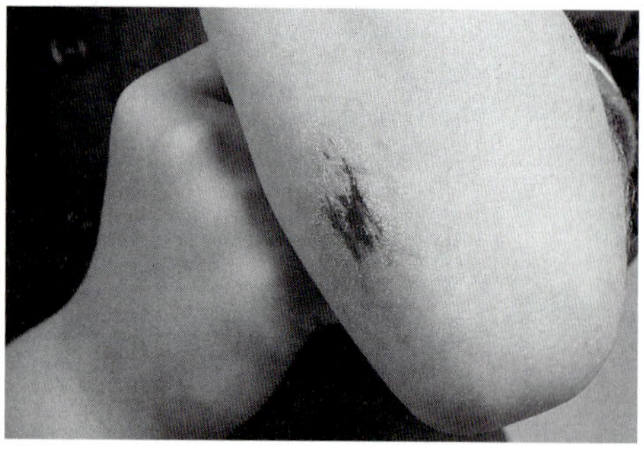

Cut

- Deep cuts can damage nerves, large blood vessels, and other soft tissues.
- Cuts bleed freely, and deep cuts can bleed severely.

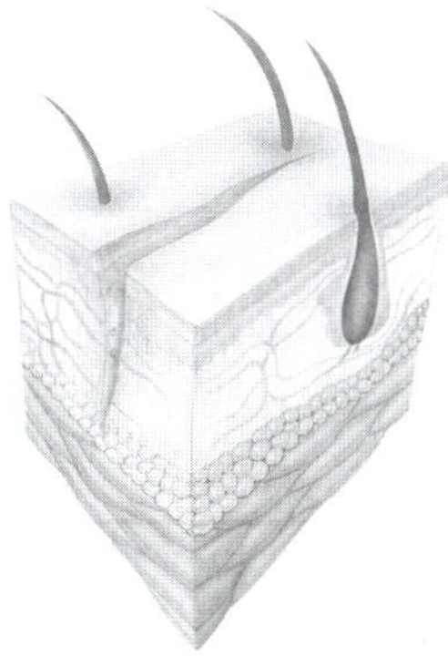

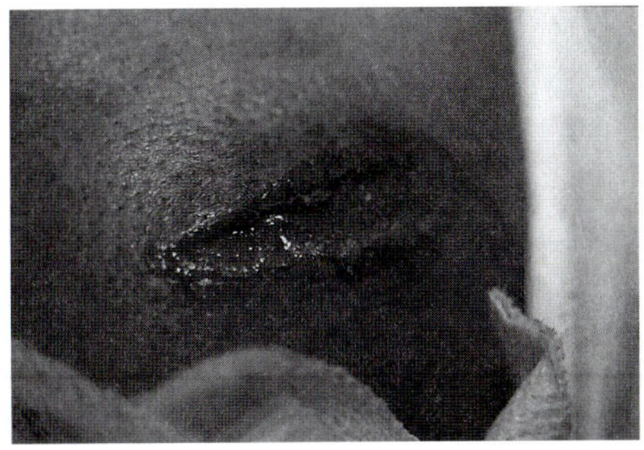

Avulsion

- An avulsion is a cut in which a piece of soft tissue or even part of the body such as a finger, is torn loose or is torn off entirely (i.e., amputation).
- Often deeper tissues are damaged, causing significant bleeding.

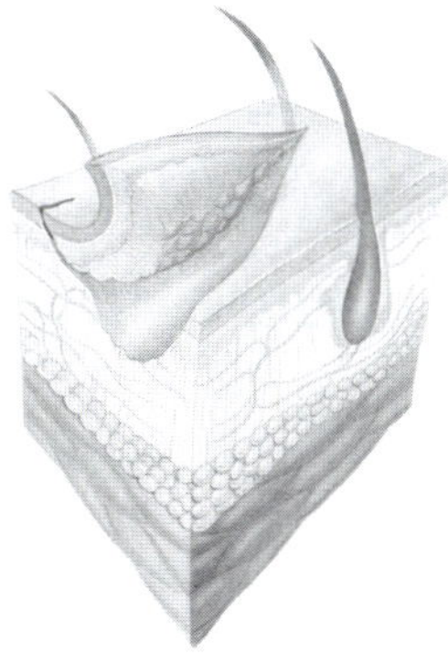

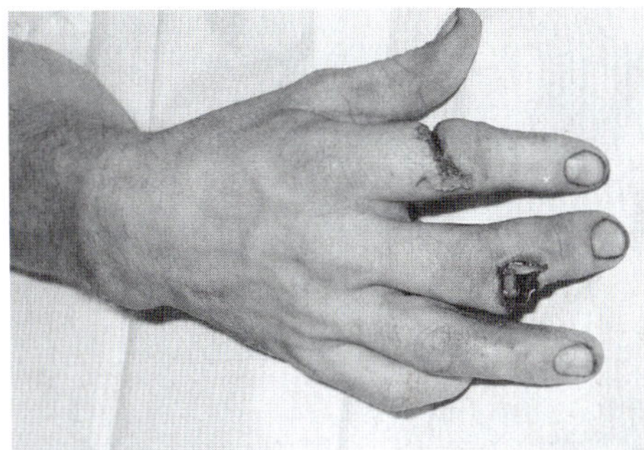

Puncture

- Puncture wounds often do not bleed a lot and can easily become infected.
- Bleeding can be severe with damage to major blood vessels or internal organs.
- An embedded object in the wound should only be removed by qualified personnel.

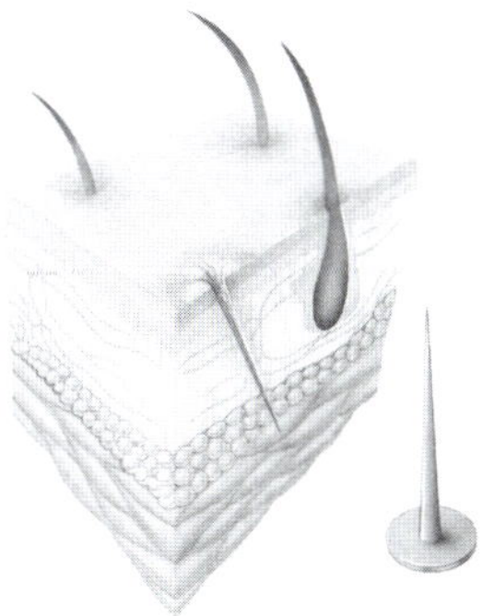

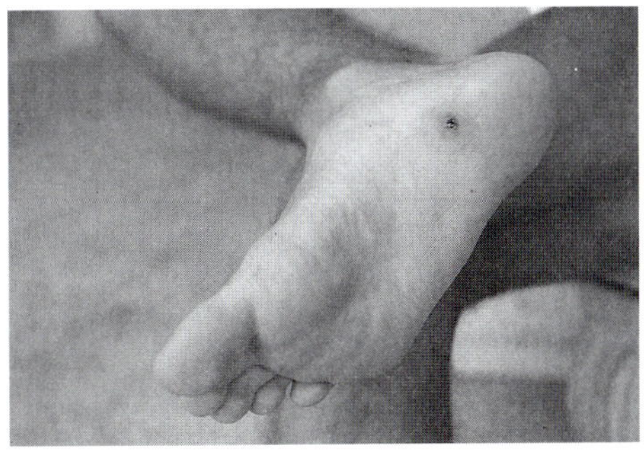

EXTERNAL BLEEDING

- Most minor bleeding stops by itself in time or by applying simple pressure.
- All bleeding needs to be controlled.

First aid to Control Bleeding

The goals of first aid are to control bleeding, prevent infection and disease transmission and minimize shock.

See the *Sport Safety Training Handbook* p. 182 for first aid steps to control bleeding.

INTERNAL BLEEDING

- Internal bleeding can be serious or life threatening.
- An injured athlete with internal bleeding needs medical help immediately.

See the *Sport Safety Training Handbook* p. 141 for the signals of internal bleeding and first aid steps.

SHOCK

- Shock can result from any serious bleeding, external or internal.
- Shock is a life-threatening condition.

See the *Sport Safety Training Handbook* p. 158 for the signals of shock and first aid steps.

SKILL PRACTICE

Use the skill sheet on the following pages to guide your practice of the skill of controlling bleeding.

SKILL SHEET

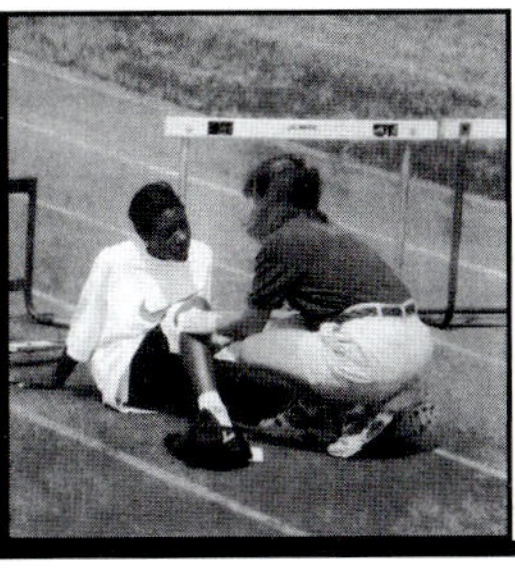

CONTROLLING BLEEDING

***CHECK** the scene for safety. **CHECK** the injured athlete, following standard precautions. **CALL** 9-1-1 or the local emergency number if necessary. To **CARE** for an athlete who is bleeding—*

STEP 1

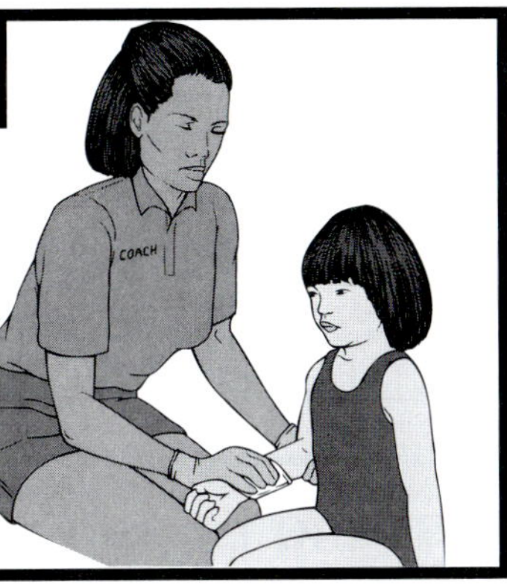

Cover the wound with a dressing and press firmly against the wound with a gloved hand.

STEP 2

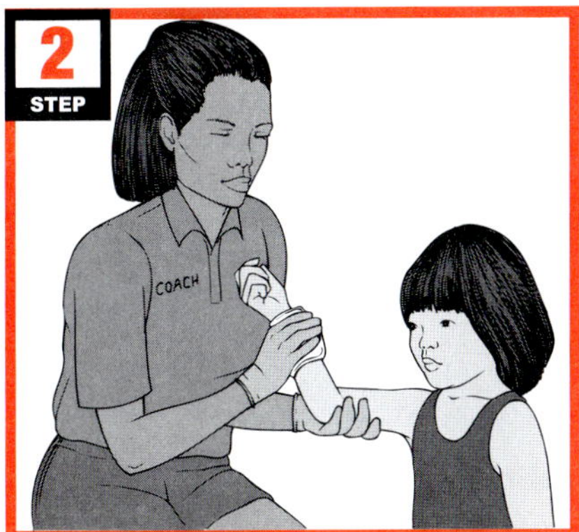

Elevate the injured area above the level of the heart if you do not suspect a broken bone.

STEP 3

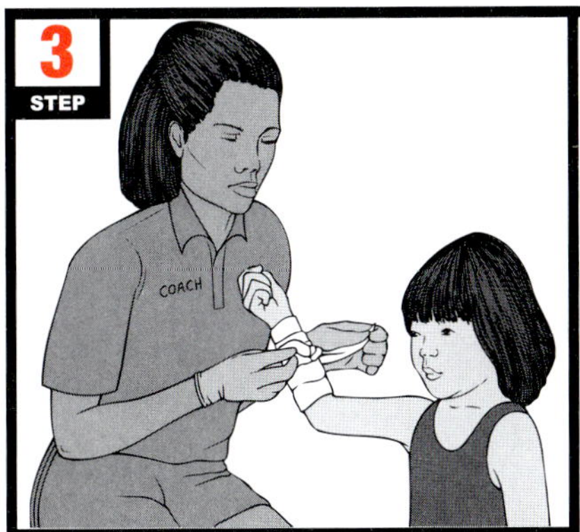

Cover dressings with a roller bandage.

Continued on next page.

CONTROLLING BLEEDING

If bleeding does not stop—

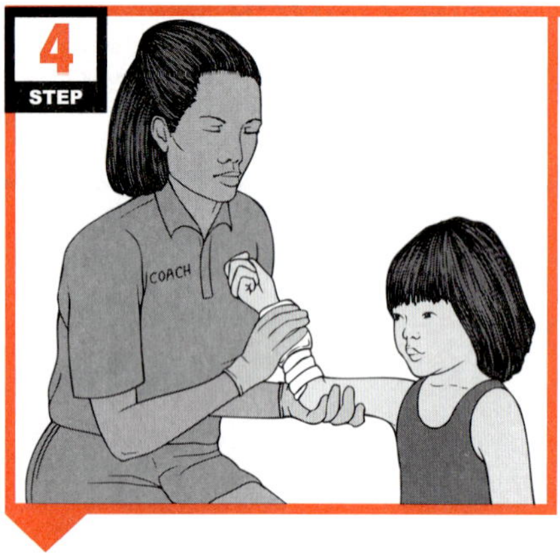

Apply additional dressings.

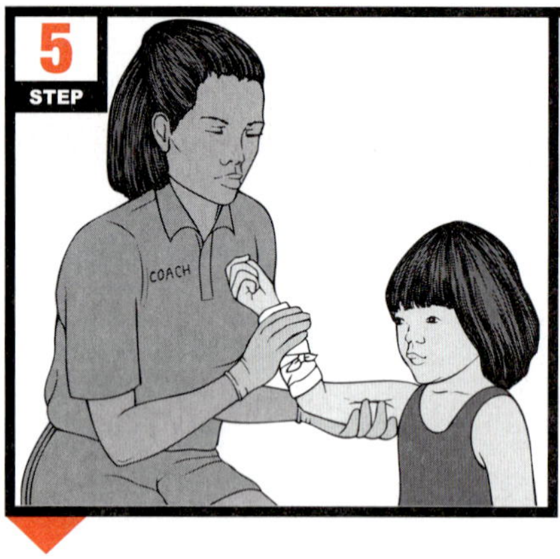

Squeeze the artery against the bone.

***Note:* If bleeding is from the leg, press with the heel of your hand where the leg bends at the hip while maintaining pressure against the wound with the other hand.**

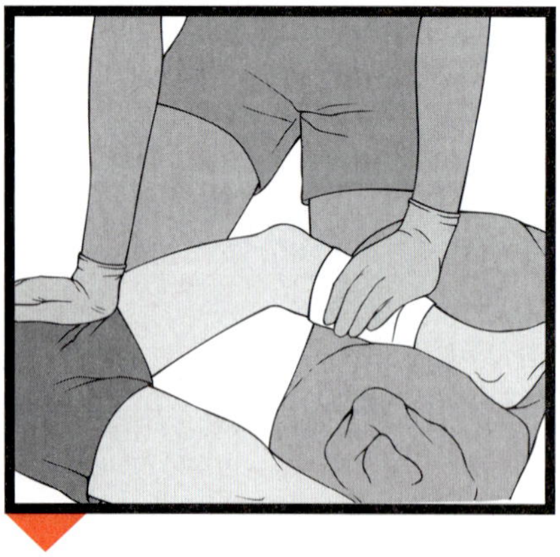

CAUSES OF BURNS

Burns are caused by—
- Heat.
- Chemicals.
- Electricity.
- Radiation.

PREVENTING BURNS

- Heat burns can be prevented by following safety practices that prevent fire and by exercising caution around sources of heat.
- Chemical burns can be prevented by following safety practices around all chemicals and by following manufacturers' guidelines whenever handling chemicals.
- Electrical burns can be prevented by following safety practices around electrical lines and equipment and by leaving outdoor areas when lightning could strike.
- Sunburn can be prevented by wearing appropriate clothing and using sunscreen. Sunscreen should have a sun protection factor (SPF) of at least 15.

See also Part 1 in the *Sport Safety Training Handbook* for safety practices.

CRITICAL BURNS

- Burns involving breathing difficulty
- Burns covering more than one body part
- Burns to the head, neck, hands, feet or genitals
- Burns (other than a very minor one) to a child or an elderly person
- Burns resulting from chemicals, explosions or electricity

A critical burn can be life threatening and needs immediate medical attention.

TYPES OF BURNS

Superficial burn (first degree)
- Involves only the top layer of skin.
- The skin is red and dry, usually painful, and the area may swell.
- Usually heals within a week without permanent scarring.

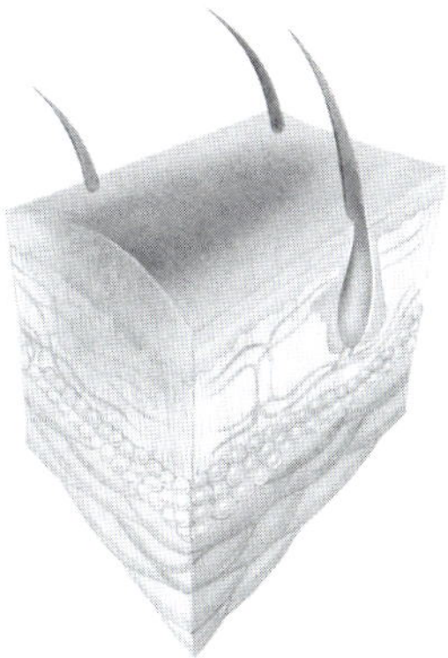

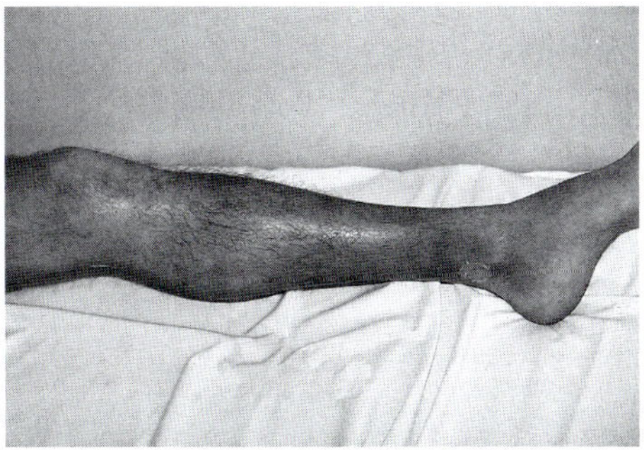

Alan Dimick, M.D., Professor of Surgery
Former Director of UAB Burn Center

Partial thickness (second degree)

- Involves the top layers of skin.
- The skin is red; usually painful; has blisters that may open and weep clear fluid, making the skin appear wet; may appear mottled; and often swells.
- Usually heals in 3 to 4 weeks and may scar.

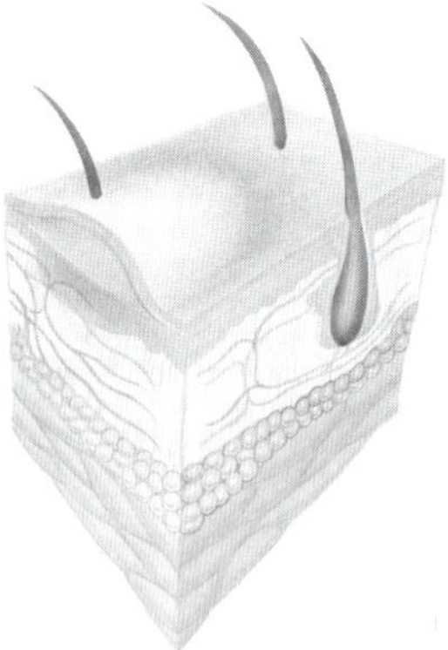

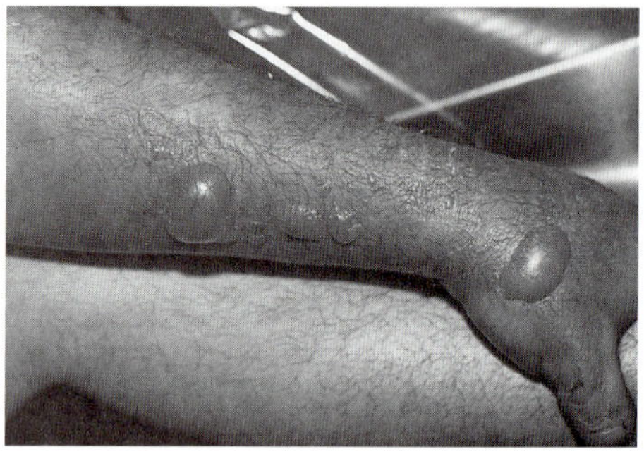

Alan Dimick, M.D., Professor of Surgery, Former Director of UAB Burn Center

Full thickness (third degree)

- May destroy all layers of skin and some or all of the underlying structures; fat, muscles, bones, and nerves.
- The skin may be brown or black (charred) with the tissues underneath sometimes appearing white and can either be extremely painful or relatively painless (if the burn destroys nerve endings).
- Healing may require medical assistance; scarring is likely.

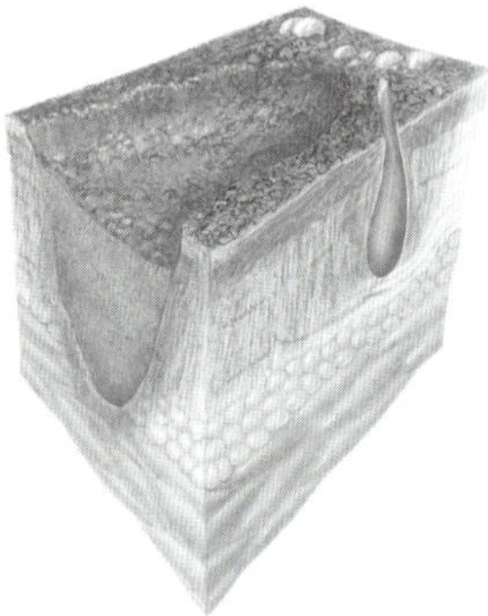

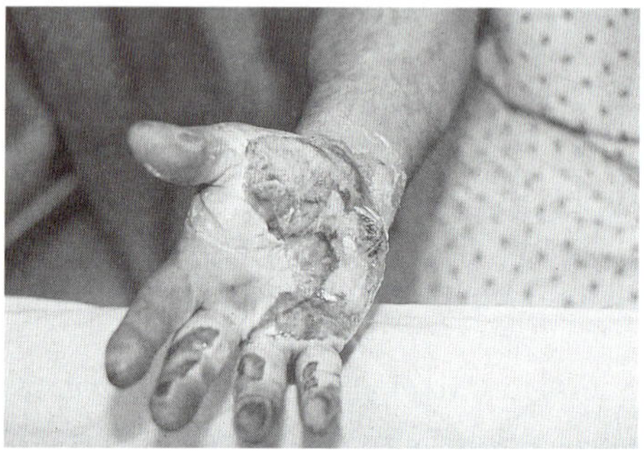

Alan Dimick, M.D., Professor of Surgery, Former Director of UAB Burn Center

FIRST AID FOR BURNS

The goals of first aid are to stop the burn, cool the burn (except electrical burns), prevent infection, and minimize shock.

Heat Burns

See the *Sport Safety Training Handbook* p. 94 for first aid steps for heat burns.

Chemical Burns

See the *Sport Safety Training Handbook* p. 98 for first aid steps for chemical burns.

Electrical Burns

See the *Sport Safety Training Handbook* p. 99 for first aid steps for electrical burns.

Radiation Burns

See the *Sport Safety Training Handbook* p. 100 for first aid steps for sunburn.

Do's and Don'ts of Burn Care

See the *Sport Safety Training Handbook* pp. 96-98.

ACTIVITIES

MATCHING

Match each term with its definition. Write its letter on the line in front of the definition.

Terms

a. shock
b. closed wound
c. avulsion
d. dressing
e. bandage
f. pressure point

Definitions

1. ____ A wound in which the skin is not broken and bleeding is internal
2. ____ A wound in which body tissue is almost torn from the body
3. ____ A site where a major artery can be squeezed closed
4. ____ Any material used to wrap or cover a body part or apply pressure
5. ____ A serious condition in which not enough blood reaches all parts of the body
6. ____ A soft pad put directly on the wound

TRUE/FALSE

Circle T if the statement is true; circle F if it is false.

1. **T** **F** Internal bleeding is not serious because the blood stays in the body.
2. **T** **F** Help keep an athlete who may be going into shock from getting chilled or overheated.
3. **T** **F** Hot, flushed skin and slow breathing are signals of shock.
4. **T** **F** For external bleeding, cover the wound with a dressing, clean cloth or the athlete's own hand before applying pressure with your hand.
5. **T** **F** For minor scrapes and cuts, first aid focuses on preventing infection.
6. **T** **F** Use a roller bandage for an arm or leg wound by wrapping it very tightly as a tourniquet.
7. **T** **F** Most chemicals continue to burn as long as they are on the skin.
8. **T** **F** A sunburn is a type of heat burn.
9. **T** **F** Deep burns can affect an athlete's ability to breathe.
10. **T** **F** Clothing reduces the seriousness of hot liquid and chemical burns.
11. **T** **F** Antibiotic ointment should be used on deep burns.
12. **T** **F** Ice is the preferred method of cooling all burns.

MULTIPLE CHOICE

Circle the answer or answers that correctly complete the following statements.

1. A full thickness (third degree) burn is—
   a. A burn in which only the top layer of skin is affected.
   b. A burn involving the top layers of skin.
   c. A burn in which all layers of skin are destroyed.
   d. A critical burn.
   e. The same as a chemical burn.
2. The severity of a burn depends on—
   a. The location of the burn on the body.
   b. The temperature of what caused the burn.
   c. The size of the burn.
   d. The position the athlete plays on the team.
   e. The length of time the athlete was burned.
3. Electrical burns may result in serious medical conditions, such as—
   a. Breathing difficulty.
   b. Fractures.
   c. Spinal injury.
   d. Unconsciousness.
   e. All of the above.

STEPS OF FIRST AID

1. Put the following first aid steps in correct order for the control of serious external bleeding. Write 1 in front of the first step to perform, 2 in front of the second step to perform, etc.
   ____ Elevate the wound above the level of the heart.
   ____ Squeeze the artery against the bone.
   ____ Press firmly against a dressing over the wound.
   ____ Cover the dressing with a bandage.
   ____ Apply more dressings.
2. Put the following first aid steps in correct order for the control of a deep burn. Write 1 in front of the first step to perform, 2 in front of the second step, etc.
   ____ Minimize shock.
   ____ Prevent infection.
   ____ Stop the burning.
   ____ Cool the burn (except electrical burns).

SCENARIOS

Imagine yourself as the coach in the following situations. You have a first aid kit and your *Sport Safety Training Handbook*. Use your *Handbook* to answer the questions for this scenario, along with information you have learned in this course.

1. A young skier loses control on the slope and strikes a tree. You check the skier and find he is lying on his side with knees bent up, barely conscious, and clutching his abdomen in pain. You do not find any external bleeding. His pulse and breathing are both rapid. Put a Y (for yes) next to the correct actions you should take in the following list and an N (for no) next to actions you should not take.
   ____ Straighten out the athlete to lie flat on his back with the legs elevated.
   ____ Send someone to call EMS personnel.
   ____ To minimize shock, keep the athlete from getting chilled.
   ____ Give the athlete lots of fluids to drink.
   ____ Try to get the athlete on his feet to walk to a warmer location.
   ____ Reassure and comfort the athlete.
2. On a very hot day, a cross-country runner has tripped and fallen to the ground. When you reach her, she is conscious and moaning with pain and her arm is bleeding profusely from a wound below the elbow. A large piece of glass protrudes from the wound.
   a. Your *immediate* goal is (circle one)
      1. Transport her to a hospital.
      2. Pull out the glass.
      3. Control the bleeding.
      4. Elevate her legs to prevent shock.
   b. You send another runner to get the first aid kit that includes dressings and bandages. While you wait for the first aid kit, you should; (circle one)
      1. Use any clean cloth as a dressing on the wound.
      2. Apply pressure on the wound around the glass.
      3. Elevate the arm.
      4. All of the above.
      5. None of the above.
   c. The other runner returns with the first aid kit. Write here what you will do with the glass in the wound:
      ____
      ____
      ____
   d. You have wrapped the wound with a roller bandage over the dressings, but blood is soaking through it. What is the next thing you should do? (circle one)
      1. Apply more dressings over the bandage.
      2. Remove the bandage and wrap it more tightly.
      3. Remove the bandage, add more dressings, and wrap the bandage again.
   e. This athlete has become confused and disoriented and is breathing rapidly, though the bleeding is now almost stopped. What additional actions should you take? (Put a "Y" [for yes] next to the correct actions you should take in the following list; write "N" [for no] next to actions you should *not* take.)
      ____ Call EMS personnel.
      ____ Reassure and calm the athlete.
      ____ Help the athlete walk back to your car.
      ____ Cover her with blankets.
      ____ Have her lie down, and elevate her legs.
      ____ Release pressure on the wound as soon as the bleeding stops.
      ____ Open the bandage and remove the glass from the wound if the athlete says it is hurting her.
3. One of your swimmers tells you that a teammate is in the locker room crying in pain and rubbing her eyes. As you enter the locker room to care for the swimmer, you smell bleach and notice that a container of disinfectant has spilled on the floor. The swimmer appears frightened and in considerable pain. (Put a "Y" [for yes] next to the actions you should take in the following list and an "N" [for no] next to actions you should *not* take.)
   ____ Delay care until you have a chance to call the Poison Control Center.
   ____ Begin flushing the swimmer's eyes with cool water.
   ____ Send someone to call EMS personnel.
   ____ Attempt to find out what the swimmer got in her eyes.
   ____ Have the swimmer stay on her feet and keep moving.
   ____ Attempt to calm and reassure the swimmer.
   ____ Pour milk on the eyes to soothe the burning.
4. After practicing all morning without a shirt, one of your tennis players complains of sunburn. His back and shoulders are hot and extremely red and painful both to touch and movement. Circle the correct answers below (more than one answer may be correct—circle all that apply).

a. Your first action(s) is (are) to—
   1. Call EMS personnel.
   2. Get the athlete out of the sun.
   3. Cool the burn, preferably with a sunburn first aid product.
b. Next, you should make sure that the athlete—
   1. Waits an hour before returning to the practice court.
   2. Stays out of the sun for at least the remainder of the day.
   3. Continues to cool the burn until the heat and pain subside.
   4. Drinks plenty of juice.

5. In the lodge after practice, a member of the bobsledding team suffers a burn while putting a log on the fire. When you go to treat the burn, you find that the spark landed on the athlete's synthetic stretch pants, melted the fabric, and left a painful, deep (second-degree) burn.
   a. What is the first action you should take? (circle one)
      1. Send someone to call EMS personnel.
      2. Pour cool water on the burn area to ensure that the burning has stopped and to cool the burn.
      3. Have the athlete remove his stretch pants.
   b. The burn has left a blister, but it is not open. How do you treat it? (circle one)
      1. Transport the athlete to a medical facility.
      2. Leave the burn area uncovered.
      3. Wash the area with soap and water, apply an antibiotic ointment, and cover it with a dry, clean dressing.
   c. What should you do the following day? (circle one)
      1. Check for signals of infection and cover the burn with a fresh dressing.
      2. Pop the blister, apply an antibiotic ointment, and cover the burn with a dry, clean dressing.
      3. Seek medical attention.

ANSWERS TO ACTIVITIES

MATCHING

1. b
2. c
3. f
4. e
5. a
6. d

TRUE/FALSE

1. F (Internal bleeding can be life-threatening, even though the blood stays inside the body.)
2. T (It is important to minimize shock by keeping an athlete from getting chilled or overheated.)
3. F (Signals of shock include pale, ashen, cool, damp skin and rapid breathing.)
4. T (Putting a barrier between the wound and your hand reduces the risk of an infection being transmitted.)
5. T (Since bleeding usually stops by itself, cleaning and covering the wound to prevent infection are most important.)
6. F (A roller bandage is used to hold the dressing in place and apply pressure on the wound; not to stop all circulation to the limb.)
7. T (Chemicals can burn a long time.)
8. F (A sunburn is a type of radiation burn.)
9. T (Deep burns can affect vital functions of the body, including breathing, in many ways.) (Most clothing does not protect the skin from being burned by hot liquids or chemicals.)
11. F (An antibiotic ointment should be used only on minor burns.)
12. F (Use ice only on minor burns; for more serious burns, use cool water.)

MULTIPLE CHOICE

1. **b, c, and d are correct** (A burn affecting only the top layer of skin is a superficial burn, and a deep burn is not the same as a chemical burn.)
2. **a, b, c, and e are all correct** (These are all factors that determine severity.)
3. **e is correct** (All of these serious medical conditions may result from an electrical burn.)

STEPS OF FIRST AID

The steps for controlling bleeding should be numbered in this order:

2 Elevate the wound above the level of the heart.
5 Squeeze the artery against the bone.
1 Press firmly against a dressing over the wound.
3 Cover the dressing with a pressure bandage.
4 Apply additional dressings.

The steps of first aid for serious burns should be numbered in this order:

4 Minimize shock;
3 Prevent infection;
1 Stop the burning;
2 Cool the burn (except electrical burns).

SCENARIOS

Scenario 1: the injured skier. This athlete may have serious internal injuries and is showing the signals of shock.

NO (Never try to move an athlete with possible broken bones or serious internal injuries. Even though elevation of the legs is appropriate in some cases of shock, never do this if the legs, hips or pelvis may be broken)

YES (Send someone to call EMS personnel. Call EMS personnel with any serious injury; it is possible internal bleeding or broken bones have occurred. This athlete needs immediate care for shock, as well.)

YES (Keep the athlete warm. Keep the athlete from getting chilled or overheated.)

NO (Do not give fluids to someone in shock or someone with possible internal injury, even though the athlete may request it.)

NO (Do not move the athlete. Wait for EMS personnel.)

YES (Reassure and comfort the athlete. Always do this for an athlete in shock. Emotional distress may make the athlete's condition worse, so try to calm him.)

Note: This skiing injury might have been preventable. The condition of the slope itself may have been responsible, or the skier may have been attempting maneuvers beyond his ability. (Some injuries may not be preventable, however. Coaching responsibilities include safety practices to prevent those that are.)

See Part 1 in the *Sport Safety Training Handbook* for injury prevention activities.

Scenario 2: the injured runner. This athlete has serious bleeding and begins to show the signals of shock.

Answer 3 is correct: you must control the bleeding first. Serious bleeding is life threatening.

Answer 4 is correct: all these actions are needed to help control the bleeding. Don't wait for the first aid kit, but use any clean cloth (or the injured athlete's own hand) to cover the wound so that you can apply pressure.

Leave the piece of glass in the wound (unless it is so loose that it is falling out) and apply bulky dressings around it. Removing an embedded object from a wound can increase the amount of bleeding.

Answer 1 is correct: Do not remove the first dressings or bandage, since this may increase the bleeding. Apply more dressings on top of the bandage.

YES (Call for EMS personnel. This athlete is going into shock from significant blood loss and needs medical attention immediately.)

YES (Reassure and calm the athlete. This helps minimize shock.)

NO (An athlete in shock should not be moved unless absolutely necessary.)

NO (Remember, it is a very hot day, and she was running. In this case it is appropriate to let her body cool to its normal temperature. The care for shock is maintaining normal body temperature, not always keeping the athlete warm.)

YES (Have her lie down, and elevate her legs. This is part of the usual care for shock.)

NO (This action should never be taken, as bleeding may start again.)

NO (Leave the embedded object in the wound to prevent renewed or increased bleeding. Explain to her why the object needs to remain in place, and comfort and reassure her that help is on the way.)

Note: This injury might have been prevented. A check of the running trail may have discovered the hazard of the broken glass, even though the fall itself may not have been preventable.

See Part 1 in the *Sport Safety Training Handbook* for injury prevention activities.

Scenario 3: Swimmer with chemical in the eyes

NO (This injury requires immediate first aid; do not delay flushing the eyes.)

YES (Flush the eyes immediately to stop the burning.)

YES (Call EMS personnel for any chemical burn.)

YES (Additional first aid may be needed.)

NO (Keep the athlete quiet and resting to minimize shock while waiting for EMS personnel.)

YES (This is standard first aid for any serious injury.)

NO (Use only water to flush the eyes to stop the burning.)

Note: This injury might have been prevented. Checking the area would have found the pool chemicals in an unsafe location.

Scenario 4: Tennis player with severe sunburn

a. First action: **2, 3** (EMS personnel are not needed for sunburn.)
b. Secondary action: **2, 3** (Preventing further burning is important, but the athlete can probably resume practice.)

Note: This burn could have easily been prevented by the use of appropriate clothing or sunscreen.

Scenario 5: Bobsledder burned by a spark

2 (Note that clothing can intensify a burn by holding the source of the burn—in this case a spark—against the skin; you need to be sure the burning has stopped and the area has cooled.)
3 (These actions are necessary to prevent infection.)
1 (Never pop blisters, that may lead to infection; keep the area covered and continue to check for signals of infection.)

11

LESSON

INJURIES TO MUSCLES, BONES AND JOINTS (MUSCULOSKELETAL)

11 LESSON

INJURIES TO MUSCLES, BONES AND JOINTS (MUSCULOSKELETAL)

PREVENTING INJURIES TO MUSCLES, BONES AND JOINTS

- Many injuries can be prevented by adopting safety practices and coaching responsibilities.
- Appropriate clothing and equipment should be worn in all practice sessions and competitions.
- Often the causes of injuries can be prevented, such as falls caused by a problem with the playing surface or improperly maintained equipment.
- Sport-specific safety practices can prevent injuries caused by personal contact with other athletes or problems with equipment, the playing surface, etc.
- Appropriate care for the injury will help prevent the injury from becoming worse.

See also Part 1 in the *Sport Safety Training Handbook* for safety practices to prevent injury.

Signals of Serious Muscle, Bone or Joint Injuries

- Pain
- Significant deformity
- Bruising and swelling
- Inability to use the affected part normally
- Bone fragments sticking out of a wound
- The injured athlete feels bones grating, felt or heard a snap or pop at the time of injury
- The injured area is cold and numb
- The cause of the injury suggests that the injury may be severe

TYPES OF INJURIES TO MUSCLES, BONES, AND JOINTS

Fracture

- Complete break, chip or crack in a bone
- Caused by fall, blow or twisting movement
- Open (open wound) or closed (skin not broken)
- Can be life threatening if it involves a large bone, such as thigh, severs an artery or affects breathing

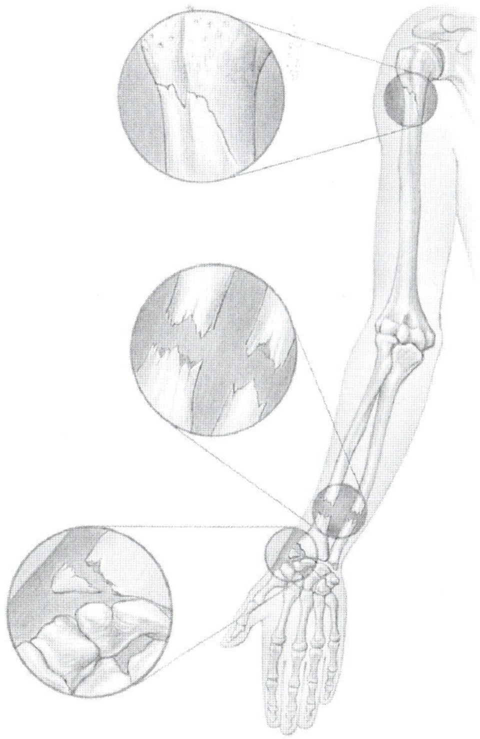

Dislocation

- Movement of a bone at a joint away from the normal position
- More obvious than a fracture
- Often forms a bump, ridge or hollow

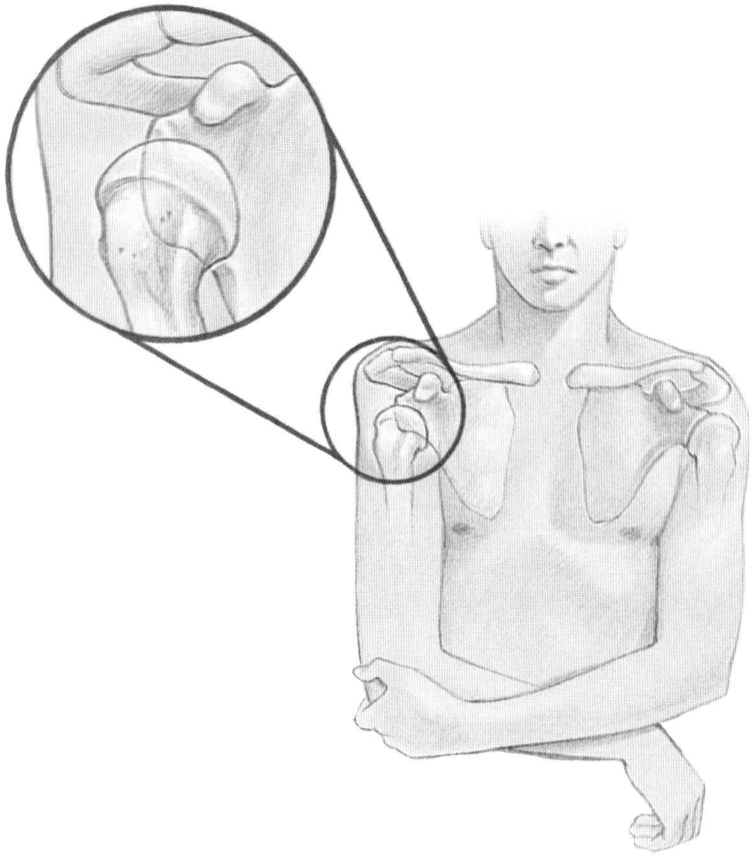

Sprain

- Tearing of ligaments at a joint
- May swell and can involve fractures or dislocations
- Most often occurs in the ankle, knee, wrist, or finger joint

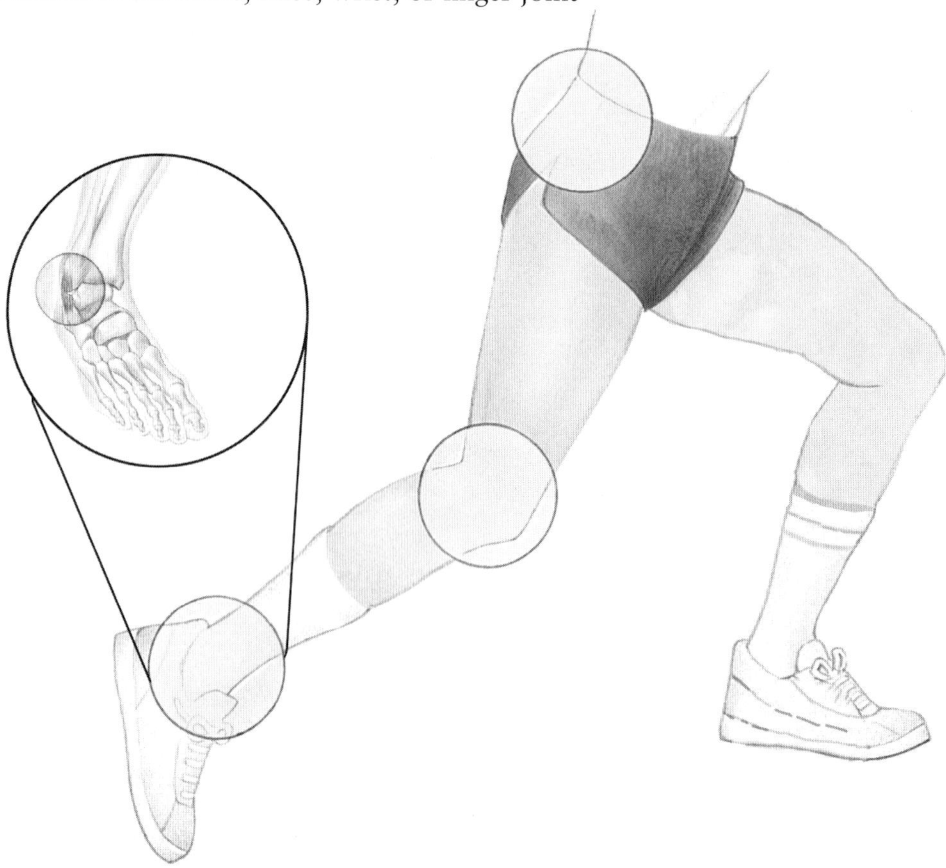

Strain

- Stretching and tearing of muscles or tendons
- Often caused by lifting or overwork
- Usually involves muscles in the neck, back, thigh, shoulder or lower leg

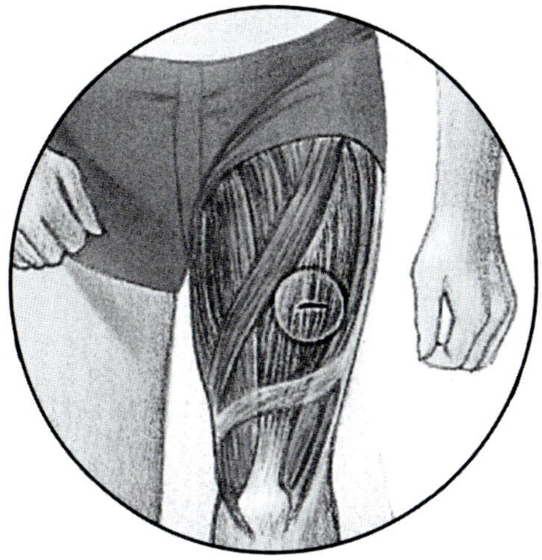

First Aid for Muscle, Bone and Joint Injuries

The goals of first aid are to react to life-threatening conditions, get help if needed, make the athlete comfortable, splint the injury if necessary, and minimize shock.

The general principles of first aid can be remembered by the acronym R.I.C.E.:

- Rest
- Immobilization
- Cold
- Elevation

NOTE: When a serious injury occurs, it is best not to move the athlete.

Fracture

See the *Sport Safety Training Handbook* p. 147 for first aid steps for Muscle, Bone and Joint (Muculoskeletal) Injuries.

Dislocation

See the *Sport Safety Training Handbook* p. 147 for first aid steps for Muscle, Bone and Joint (Muculoskeletal) Injuries.

Sprain

See the *Sport Safety Training Handbook* p. 147 for first aid steps for Muscle, Bone and Joint (Musculoskeletal) Injuries.

Strain

See the *Sport Safety Training Handbook* p. 147 for first aid steps for Muscle, Bone and Joint (Musculoskeletal) Injuries.

HEAD, NECK AND BACK INJURIES

When to Suspect Head, Neck and Back Injuries

- Significant hard contact with structures or objects, especially with the crown or top of the head
- A fall from a height greater than the athlete's height
- Any diving accident
- An athlete found unconscious for unknown reasons
- Any injury involving severe blunt force to the head or trunk, such as from a soccer collision or a Taekwondo blow
- Any injury that penetrates the head or trunk, such as track shoe spike wounds
- A motor vehicle crash involving a driver or passengers not wearing safety belts
- Any person thrown from a motor vehicle

- Any injury in which the athlete's helmet is broken, including accidents involving football, hockey, bobsledding or cycling
- Any incident involving a lightning strike

Signals of Head, Neck and Back Injuries

- Changes in consciousness
- Severe pain or pressure in the head, neck or back
- Tingling or loss of sensation in the hands, fingers, feet and toes
- Partial or complete loss of movement of any body part
- Unusual bumps or depressions on the head or over the spine
- Blood or other fluids in the ears or nose
- Heavy external bleeding from the head, neck or back
- Seizures
- Impaired breathing or vision as a result of injury
- Nausea or vomiting
- Persistent headache
- Loss of balance
- Bruising of the head, especially around the eyes and behind the ears

General Care for Head, Neck and Back Injuries

- Minimize movement of the head, neck, and back.
- Maintain an open airway.
- Check consciousness and breathing.
- Control any external bleeding.
- To minimize shock, keep the athlete from getting chilled or overheated.
- Do not move the athlete until EMS personnel arrive.

First Aid for Head, Neck or Back Injuries

See the *Sport Safety Training Handbook* p. 135

SPLINTING

- If you must move or transport the athlete, you should splint the injured part.
- By applying a splint, you can help minimize movement and further injury.

When and How to Splint

- Splint only if you can do it without causing more pain and discomfort to the athlete.
- Splint an injury in the position you find it.
- Splint the injured area and the joints above and below the injured part.
- Check for proper circulation before and after splinting to ensure that the splint or bandages have not been applied too tightly.

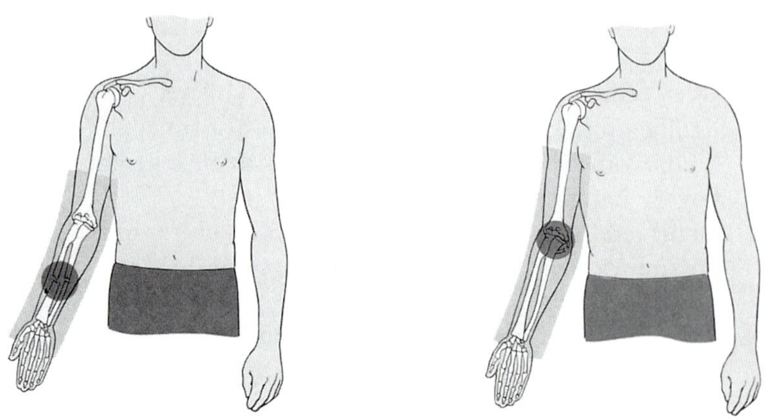

- **SKILL PRACTICE**

Use the skill sheets on the following pages to guide your practice of splinting skills.

APPLY AN ANATOMIC SPLINT

***CHECK** the scene for safety. **CHECK** the injured athlete, following standard precautions as appropriate. **CALL** 9-1-1 or the local emergency number if necessary. To **CARE** for an athlete who has an injured limb—*

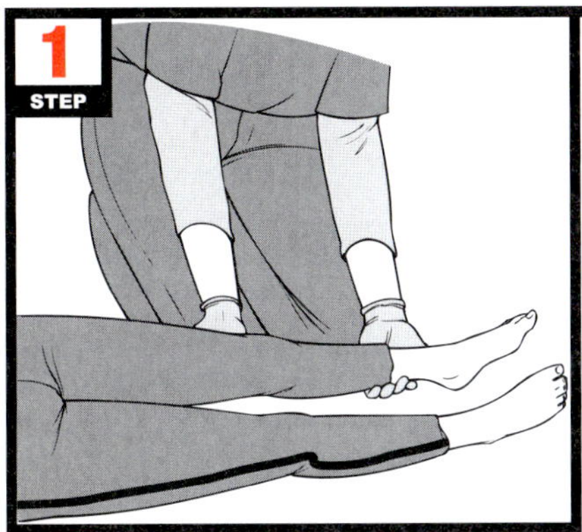

Support the injured area above and below the site of the injury.

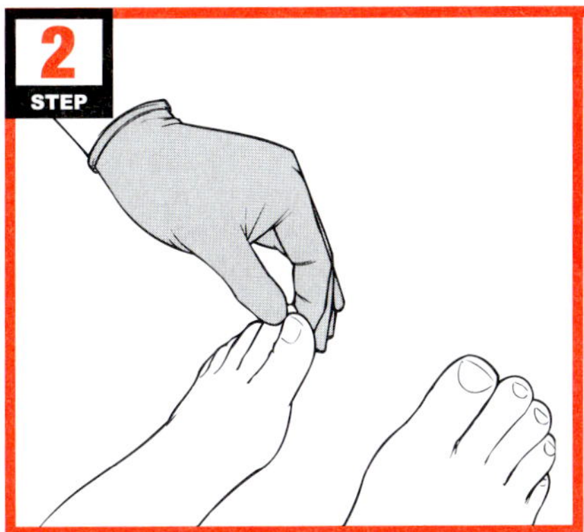

Check for feeling, warmth and color.

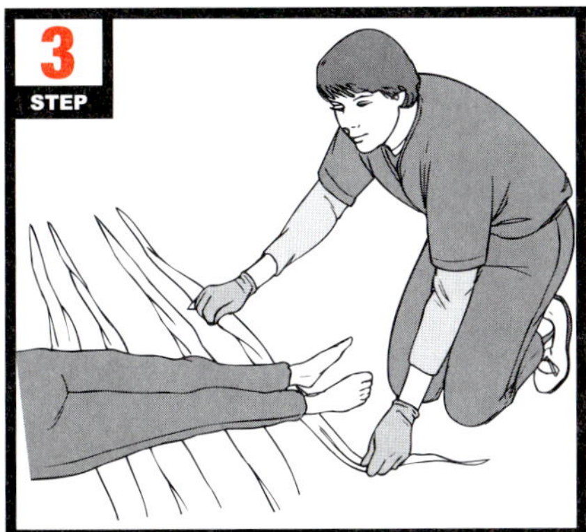

Place several folded triangular bandages above and below the injured area.

Continued on next page.

APPLY AN ANATOMIC SPLINT

Place the uninjured area next to the injured area.

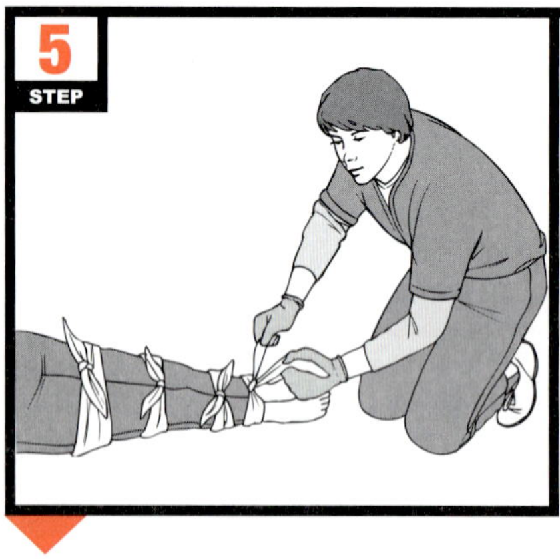

Tie triangular bandages securely.

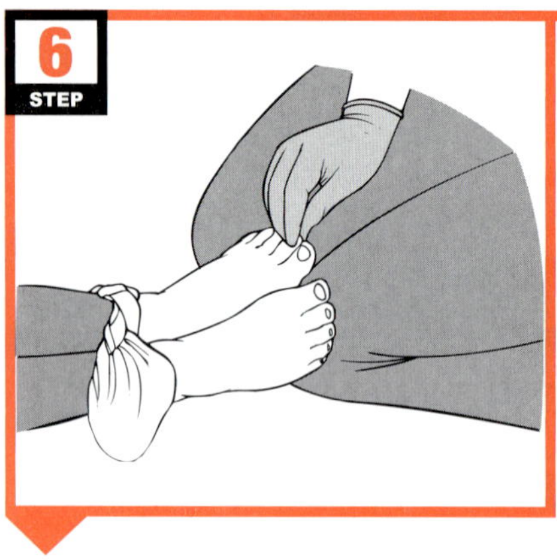

Recheck for feeling, warmth and color.

If you are not able to check warmth and color because a sock or shoe is in place, check for feeling.

APPLY A SOFT SPLINT

***CHECK** the scene for safety. **CHECK** the injured athlete, following standard precautions as appropriate. **CALL** 9-1-1 or the local emergency number if necessary. To **CARE** for an athlete who has an injured limb—*

1 STEP

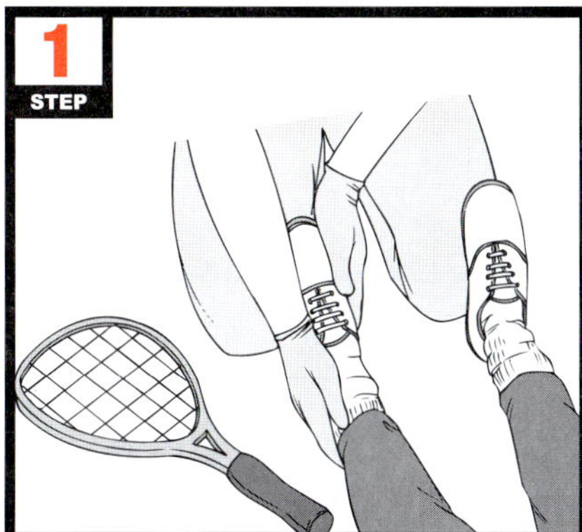

Support the injured area above and below the site of the injury.

2 STEP

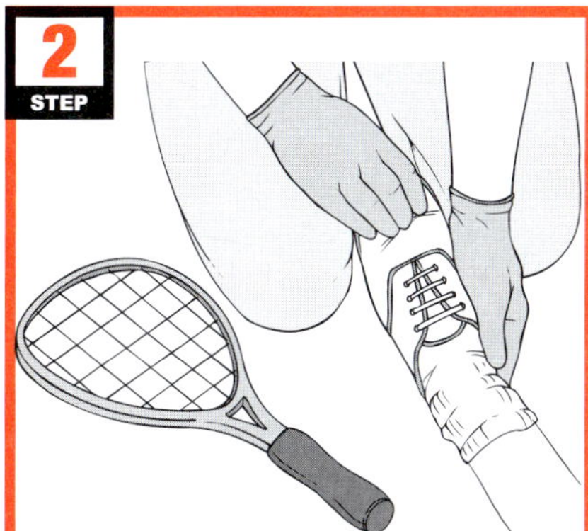

Check for feeling, warmth and color.

3 STEP

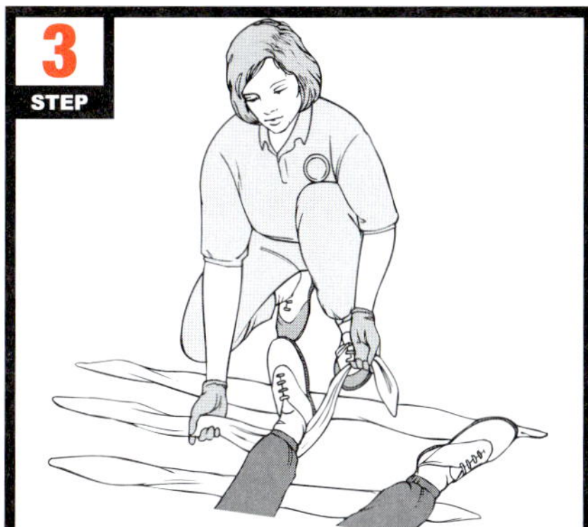

Place several folded triangular bandages above and below the injured area.

Continued on next page.

APPLY A SOFT SPLINT

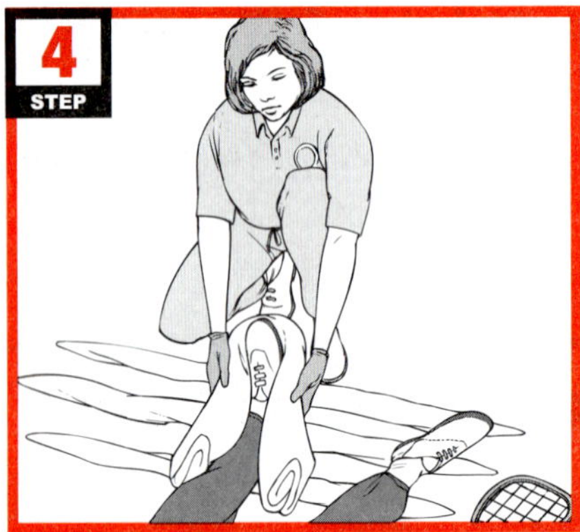

Gently wrap a soft object (a folded blanket or a pillow) around the injured area.

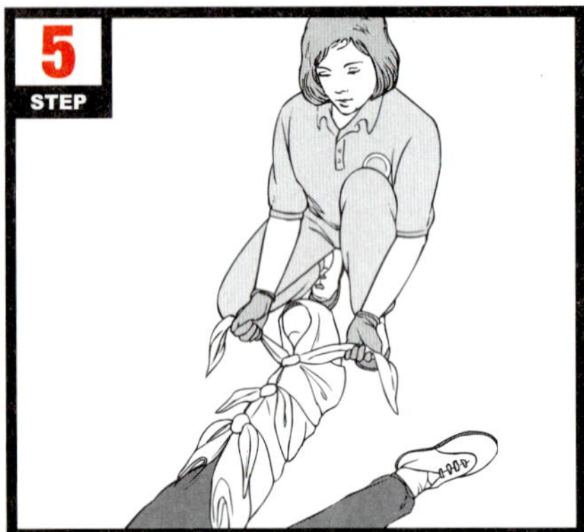

Tie triangular bandages securely.

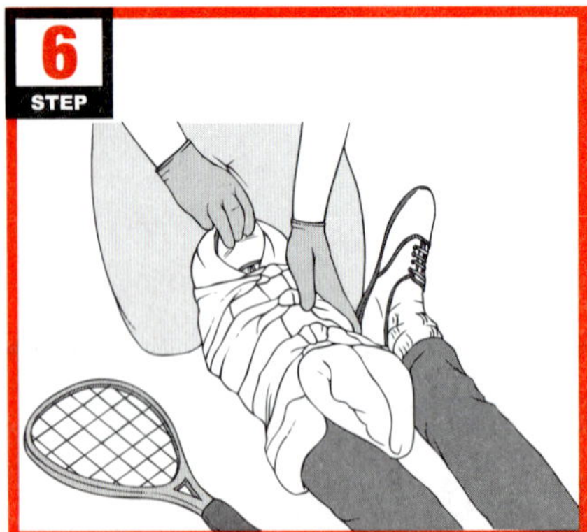

Recheck for feeling, warmth and color.

If you are not able to check warmth and color because a sock or shoe is in place, check for feeling.

APPLY A SLING

***CHECK** the scene for safety. **CHECK** the injured athlete, following standard precautions as appropriate. **CALL** 9-1-1 or the local emergency number if necessary. To **CARE** for an athlete who has an injured limb—*

STEP 1

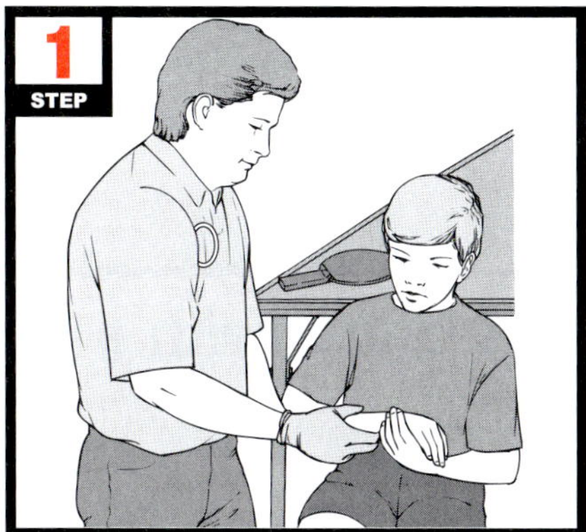

Support the injured area above and below the site of the injury.

STEP 2

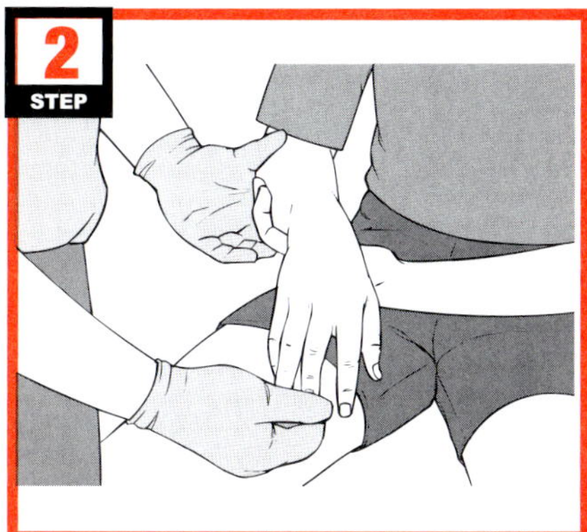

Check for feeling, warmth and color.

STEP 3

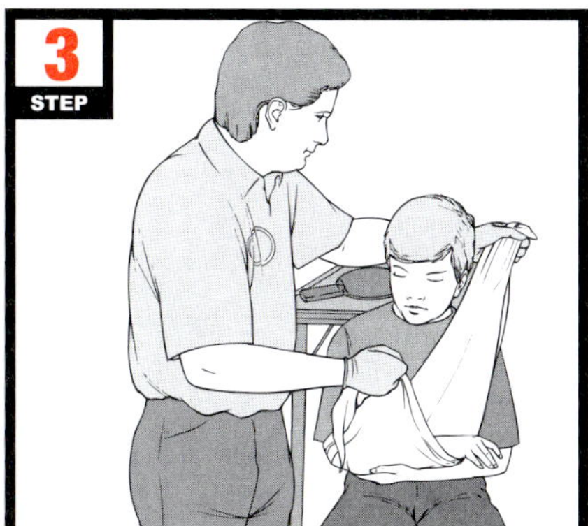

Place a triangular bandage under the injured arm and over the uninjured shoulder to form a sling.

Continued on next page.

SKILL SHEET

APPLY A SLING

4
STEP

Tie the ends of the sling at the side of the neck.

5
STEP

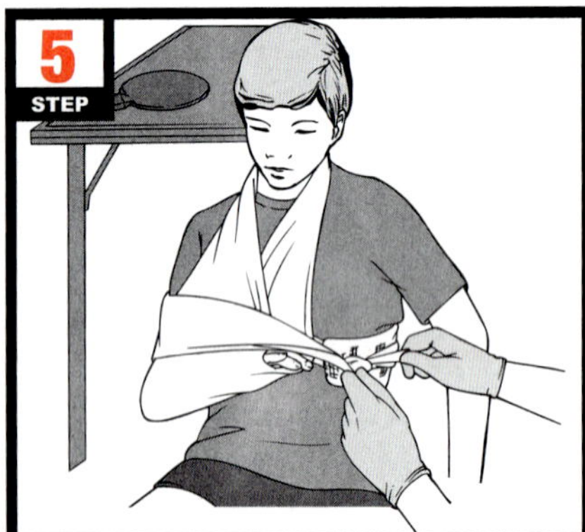

Bind the injured area to the chest with a folded triangular bandage.

6
STEP

Recheck for feeling, warmth and color.

SKILL SHEET

APPLY A RIGID SPLINT

***CHECK** the scene for safety. **CHECK** the injured athlete, following standard precautions as appropriate. **CALL** 9-1-1 or the local emergency number if necessary. To **CARE** for an athlete who has an injured limb—*

1 STEP

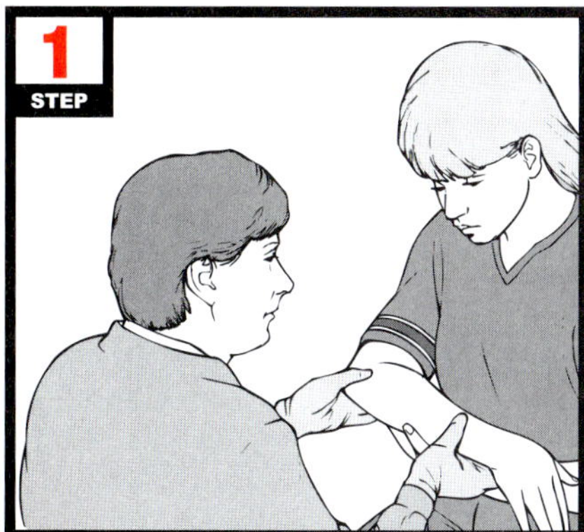

Support the injured area above and below the site of the injury.

2 STEP

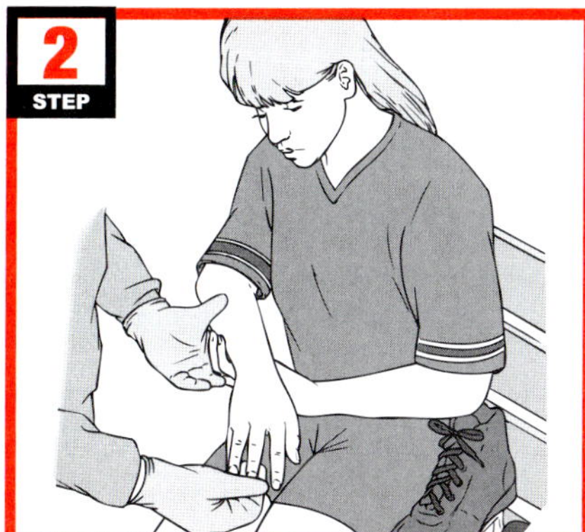

Check for feeling, warmth and color.

3 STEP

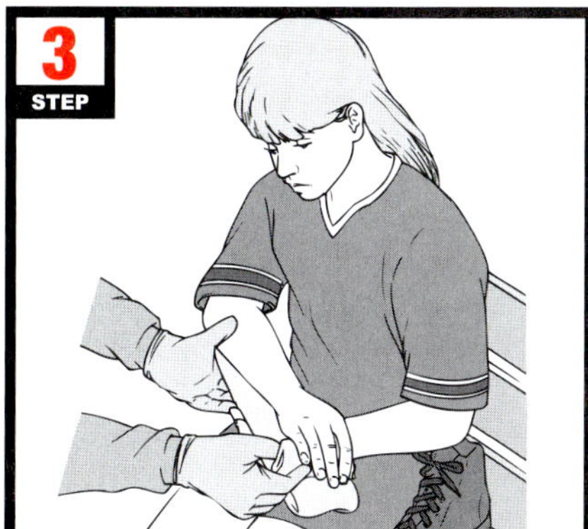

Place the rigid splint (board) under the injured area and the joints that are above and below the injured area.

Continued on next page.

SKILL SHEET

APPLY A RIGID SPLINT

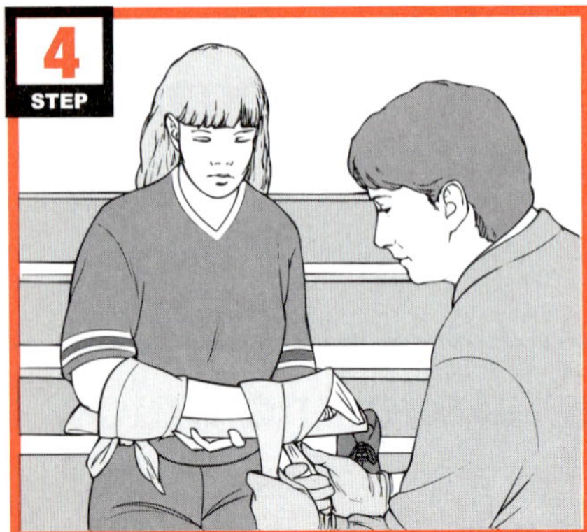

STEP 4

Tie several folded triangular bandages above and below the injured area.

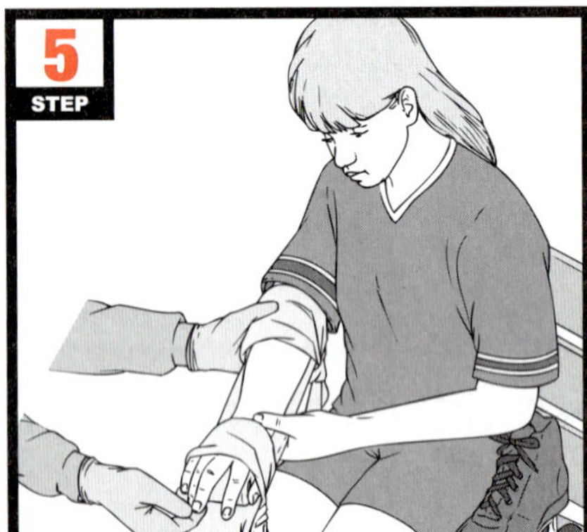

STEP 5

Recheck for feeling, warmth and color.

If a rigid splint is used on a forearm, you must also immobilize the elbow. Bind the arm to the chest using folded triangular bandages or apply a sling.

ACTIVITIES

MULTIPLE CHOICE

Circle the answer or answers that correctly complete the following statements

1. Generally, a fracture can be life threatening if it—
   a. Involves more than one limb.
   b. Severs an artery.
   c. Affects breathing.
   d. Results from a motor vehicle accident.
   e. Involves large bones, such as the thigh.
2. Suspect a serious muscle, bone or joint injury if—
   a. The athlete experiences considerable pain.
   b. The injured area is warm.
   c. The injured area is bruised and swelling.
   d. The injured athlete felt or heard a "snap" or "pop" at the time of the injury.
3. Indications that head and spinal injury have occurred include—
   a. Diving injuries.
   b. Injuries in which safety helmets are broken.
   c. Lightning strikes.
   d. Falls from heights greater than the athlete's height.
   e. Motor vehicle injuries with the athlete not wearing a safety belt.

TRUE/FALSE

Circle T if the statement is true; circle F if it is false.

1. **T F** The four basic types of injuries to muscles, bones, and joints are fractures, dislocations, sprains and strains.
2. **T F** Dislocations are not as obvious as fractures.
3. **T F** Fractures can be open (open wound) or closed (skin is not broken).
4. **T F** Caring for a muscle, bone or joint injury requires knowing exactly what type of injury has occurred.
5. **T F** Head, neck and back injuries should always be treated as though they are serious.

STEPS OF FIRST AID

Put the following first aid steps in correct order for the response to a suspected serious muscle, bone or joint injury. Write 1 in front of the first step to perform, 2 in front of the second step, etc.

____ Send someone to call EMS personnel, if necessary.
____ Check and care for life-threatening conditions.
____ Splint the suspected injury, if necessary.
____ Minimize shock.
____ Make the athlete comfortable.

SCENARIOS

Imagine yourself as the coach in the following situations. You have a first aid kit and your *Sport Safety Training Handbook*. Use your *Handbook* to answer the questions for this scenario, along with information you have learned in this course.

1. A member of the field hockey team stumbles and falls to the ground after making a hard shot on goal. When you reach her, she is lying on her side, holding her left knee and grimacing in pain. (Place a "Y" [for yes] next to actions you should take in the following list and an "N" [for no] next to actions you should *not* take.)
   ____ Take a few minutes to try to determine if she has a fracture, dislocation, sprain or strain.
   ____ Check for life-threatening conditions.
   ____ Calm the athlete and attempt to make her comfortable.
   ____ Use signals such as pain, deformity, and her ability to use the leg to decide whether to send someone to call EMS personnel.
   ____ Slowly help her straighten out her injured leg, then splint it.
2. A member of the luge team loses control of his sled as he comes out of the final turn and somersaults along the course toward the finish. You and a number of spectators reach the injured competitor first. The athlete is crumpled on his stomach, lying still; his helmet has come off, his head has minor bleeding, and one of his arms is twisted unnaturally. What should you do while waiting for medical personnel to arrive?

____
____
____
____

ANSWERS TO ACTIVITIES

MULTIPLE CHOICE

1. **b, c, and e are correct** (A fracture can be life threatening if an artery is severed, breathing is affected, or a large bone is broken. Fractures involving two limbs or resulting from an automobile accident are not automatically life threatening.)
2. **a, c, and d are correct** (Considerable pain, bruising and swelling, and a snapping or popping sound are all signals of a serious injury; warmth in the area is not.)
3. **a, b, c, d, and e are correct** (All of the factors listed here may be signals of a head, neck or back injury.)

TRUE/FALSE

1. T (The listed four types are all musculoskeletal injuries, but you do not have to diagnose a particular type of injury before giving first aid.)
2. F (Dislocations can be obvious also because deformity may result.)
3. T (All fractures are either open or closed.)
4. F (Regardless of the type of musculoskeletal injury, you do not have to diagnose a particular type of injury before giving first aid.)
5. T (Always assume a head, neck or back injury is serious; acting as if the injury is not serious may lead to further injury and permanent disability.)

STEPS OF FIRST AID

The steps should be numbered in this order:

2 Send someone to call EMS personnel, if necessary;
1 Check and care for life-threatening conditions;
4 Splint the suspected injury, if necessary;
5 Minimize shock;
3 Make the athlete comfortable.

SCENARIOS

Scenario 1: Field hockey player with injured knee

a. **NO** (Don't waste the time, because the basic first aid for fracture, dislocation, sprain or strain is the same.)
b. **YES** (Always check for life-threatening injuries.)
c. **YES** (Calming an injured athlete helps ease pain, encourages resting the injured area **and** preventing further damage, and reduces the possibility of shock.)
d. **YES** (The decision to call EMS personnel depends on the severity of the injury; look for these signals of a serious injury.)
e. **NO** (Support the limb with towels, jackets, etc., to allow the athlete to keep it in the most comfortable position possible.)

Note: Could this injury have been prevented? That depends, of course, on its cause. If some irregularity in the field surface caused the player to trip, the fall could have been prevented by checking the playing surface before the practice. If the player fell because the knee had been injured earlier in the practice but the player had returned to play, the injury could have been prevented by having the player sit out or seeking medical attention earlier. See Part 1 of the *Sport Safety Training Handbook* for a discussion of injury prevention.

Scenario 2: Injured luge athlete

a. Assume the athlete has multiple injuries, including a head injury, a possible spine injury, and a fractured arm. While waiting for medical personnel, your immediate actions should be—
   - Caution other people not to touch the athlete.
   - Without moving him, try to determine if he is breathing, if he is conscious, and if he has any external bleeding in addition to the head wound.
   - If he is conscious, calmly tell him to lie still and reassure him that help is coming.

Note: Although the accident may not have been preventable, the possible head injury might have been prevented or minimized. The helmet should not have come off. The equipment may have been faulty, or the player may not have correctly fastened it always check for equipment problems. Remind your athletes to use equipment properly. See Part 1 of the *Sport Safety Training Handbook* for a discussion of injury prevention.

12
LESSON

SUDDEN ILLNESS

12
LESSON

SUDDEN ILLNESS

TYPES OF SUDDEN ILLNESS

- Seizure
- Stroke
- Diabetic Emergencies
- Fainting
- Vomiting
- Poisoning
- Bites and Stings
- Heat-Related Emergencies
- Cold-Related Emergencies

PREVENTING SUDDEN ILLNESS

- Some sudden illnesses may be prevented by seeking medical attention at the first signals of a problem.
- A diabetic emergency may be prevented by following the physician's instructions for diet, use of insulin and activity.
- Poisoning may be prevented by avoiding direct or indirect contact with poisonous substances and not misusing or abusing substances for inappropriate purposes.
- Bites and stings may be prevented by taking care to avoid contact with insects and animals in settings where such contact may be possible.
- Heat-related emergencies may be prevented by following safety guidelines for activity in hot environments (**see the *Sport Safety Training Handbook* p.** 25).
- Cold-related emergencies (frostbite and hypothermia), may be prevented by following safety guidelines for clothing and activity in cold environments (**see the *Sport Safety Training Handbook* p.** 27).
- Appropriate care for the illness will help prevent it from becoming worse.
- Coaches should be aware of potentially susceptible athletes by reviewing athletes' medical information.

See also Lesson 1 of this workbook and Part 1 in the *Sport Safety Training Handbook* for safety practices to prevent illness and injury.

SIGNALS OF SUDDEN ILLNESS

- There are many types of sudden illness, but they often have similar signals.
- In most cases, you do not need to try to determine the specific sudden illness before giving first aid.

See the *Sport Safety Training Handbook* p. 165 for the signals of sudden illness.

FIRST AID FOR SUDDEN ILLNESS

- You do not need to know the exact cause of sudden illness to provide the proper initial care. Only in a few situations—such as seizure, vomiting, poisoning or known diabetic emergency—does your care require you to do more if you do know the cause of the illness.

See the *Sport Safety Training Handbook* p. 166 for first aid steps.

WHEN TO CALL EMS PERSONNEL

See the *Sport Safety Training Handbook* p. 166 for when to call EMS personnel in cases of sudden illness.

SPECIFIC ILLNESSES

Seizure

- Irregular electrical activity of the brain, caused by injury, disease, fever or infection.
- May be caused by epilepsy, a chronic condition.
- Ranges from mild blackouts to sudden, uncontrolled muscular contractions (convulsions) that last several minutes.
- Some people experience an "aura" before a seizure—an unusual sensation or feeling.

Stroke

- A condition in which a part of the brain does not receive enough blood, causing sudden changes in the brain's activity.
- Some signals are similar to many sudden illnesses.
- Some signals, such as sudden inability to move a body part or sudden paralysis, may occur on only one side of the body.

Diabetic Emergency

- The body is unable to properly convert sugar from food into energy.
- Signals of a diabetic emergency include changes in the level of consciousness, rapid breathing and pulse and feeling and looking ill.

Fainting

- Fainting is a temporary loss of consciousness caused by an insufficient supply of blood to the brain.
- A person who faints usually recovers quickly and suffers no lasting effects.
- A person about to faint often becomes pale or ashen and begins to perspire.
- Lying or sitting with the head level with the knees can sometimes prevent a fainting spell.

Vomiting

- Vomiting can be a signal of a serious illness.
- Most important, turn a vomiting person on her or his side to keep the airway clear.

Poisoning

- Poisoning can occur by ingestion, inhalation, absorption or injection.
- If you think someone has been poisoned, call the National Poison Control Center at (800) 222-1222. For any life-threatening condition (such as an unsafe scene, an athlete who is unconscious or is having trouble breathing or having seizures), call 9-1-1 or the local emergency number, or have someone else call if possible.

Bites and Stings

- Insect stings can be painful but rarely fatal, although some people may experience severe allergic reactions.
- There are only two spiders in the United States whose bite can cause illness or death, the black widow and the brown recluse.
- Lyme disease is an illness that is contracted from the bite of an infected tick.

Heat-related Emergencies

- Heat-related emergencies include heat cramps, heat exhaustion and heat stroke.
- Heat stroke can result in death.
- Athletes often keep training or competing after they begin to feel ill.
- Once the signals of a heat-related emergency begin to appear, the athlete's condition can worsen quickly.

Cold-related Emergencies

- Cold-related emergencies include frostbite and hypothermia.
- Cold-related emergencies can result in death.
- Athletes often keep training or competing after they begin to feel ill.
- Once the signals of cold-related emergencies begin to appear, the athlete's condition can worsen quickly.

ACTIVITIES

MULTIPLE CHOICE

Circle the answer or answers that correctly complete the following statements.

1. Common signals of sudden illness include—
   a. Feeling lightheaded, dizzy, confused or weak.
   b. Looking pale, ashen or flushed.
   c. Extreme hunger.
   d. Nausea, vomiting or diarrhea.
   e. Sweating.
2. Other signals of sudden illness include—
   a. Unconsciousness.
   b. Breathing difficulty.
   c. Seizure, paralysis or inability to move.
   d. Slurred speech or difficulty seeing.
3. When responding to sudden illness, always call EMS personnel if the athlete—
   a. Has fainted.
   b. Has injuries to the head, neck or back.
   c. Complains of not feeling well.
   d. Vomits.
   e. Has persistent chest pain or pressure.
   f. Has been in contact with a poisonous plant.
4. Always call EMS personnel for a seizure if—
   a. The athlete is a child.
   b. The seizure lasts more than a few minutes or is followed by more seizures.
   c. The athlete is pregnant.
   d. The athlete is a diabetic.
   e. The athlete has had seizures before.
   f. The athlete does not regain consciousness.
5. Toxic fumes that can cause poisoning include—
   a. Carbon monoxide from engine or car exhaust.
   b. Chlorine from swimming pool products.
   c. Glue.
   d. Cleaning materials.
6. Poisons that can be absorbed through the skin include—
   a. Poison ivy, poison oak and poison sumac.
   b. Crack cocaine.
   c. Some chemicals, such as the fertilizers and pesticides used on playing fields.
   d. All toxic fumes.
7. In addition to exposure to temperature extremes, the likelihood of heat- or cold-related emergencies depends on—
   a. An athlete's age and health.
   b. Wind and humidity.
   c. Clothing.
   d. Physical activity.
8. Heat-related emergencies include—
   a. Heat stroke.
   b. Heat cramps.
   c. Heat exhaustion.
   d. Sunburn.
9. Cold-related emergencies include—
   a. Muscle cramps.
   b. Upset stomach.
   c. Frostbite.
   d. Hypothermia.
10. The likelihood of heat- or cold-related emergencies is increased for athletes who—
    a. Have glaucoma.
    b. Have poor circulation.
    c. Take diuretics.
    d. Are very young or very old.
11. Signals of frostbite include—
    a. White, yellow or blue skin.
    b. Red, raw skin.
    c. Numbness.
    d. Waxy, cold skin.
    e. Fingers feel cold.
12. Signals of hypothermia include—
    a. Numbness.
    b. Hyperactivity.
    c. Glassy stare and apathy.
    d. Loss of consciousness.
    e. Shivering.

MATCHING

Match each term with its definition. Write its letter on the line in front of the definition.

Terms

a. Frostbite
b. Antibiotics
c. Hypothermia
d. Carbon dioxide
e. Heat cramps
f. Heat stroke
g. Antivenin
h. Heat exhaustion

Definitions

1. _____ Cooling of the entire body
2. _____ A severe heat-related emergency characterized by red, hot, dry skin; changes in consciousness; rapid, weak pulse; and rapid, shallow breathing

3. _____ Medication that blocks the effects of poison, such as from a spider bite or scorpion sting
4. _____ A heat-related emergency characterized by painful muscle spasms, generally in the legs and abdomen, that indicate that the body is having trouble with the heat
5. _____ Toxic gas from wells and sewers
6. _____ Serious heat-related emergency characterized by cool, moist, pale or ashen or flushed skin; headache; nausea; dizziness; weakness; and exhaustion
7. _____ Freezing of body parts exposed to the cold
8. _____ Medication used to treat Lyme's disease

TRUE/FALSE

Circle T if the statement is true; circle F if it is false.

1. T F The environment—such as extreme heat or cold— can be a clue to the cause of sudden illness.
2. T F You should not attempt to provide first aid for sudden illness unless you positively know the cause.
3. T F If the athlete vomits, position the athlete on her or his side to keep the airway clear.
4. T F A stroke can be a cause of sudden illness.
5. T F Do not give food or drink to an athlete who has fainted.
6. T F If a known diabetic does not feel better 5 minutes after taking sugar, you should call EMS personnel.
7. T F Poisoning deaths among adults 18 and over have increased in recent years due to suicides and drug use.
8. T F In a poisoning emergency, you should call only 9-1-1.
9. T F If an athlete who has been poisoned vomits, quickly discard the vomit to ensure that others do not come in contact with it.
10. T F The skin color of someone who has breathed toxic fumes may turn pale, ashen or bluish due to a lack of oxygen.
11. T F Insect stings can cause a severe allergic reaction, which can result in a breathing emergency.
12. T F Never remove an insect stinger.
13. T F Lyme disease signals begin within hours of a bite from an infected deer tick.
14. T F For a snakebite, wash the wound, immobilize the injured area and keep it lower than the heart if possible.
15. T F Get medical attention immediately if an athlete is bitten by an animal and rabies is suspected.
16. T F Temperature, time of day and wind are the three main factors affecting body temperature.
17. T F Once the signals of a heat- or cold-related emergency begin to appear, the worst is over.
18. T F Cooling the large blood vessels by applying ice or cold packs to an athlete's wrists and ankles, on the groin, in the armpits and on the neck is advisable for severe heat-related emergencies.
19. T F Hypothermia only occurs when the temperature drops below freezing.
20. T F Aggressively rub body parts that appear to be frostbitten.

FILL-IN-THE–BLANKS

1. If you know an athlete has a medical condition, you can provide more specific care than if you do not know the cause of sudden illness. These medical conditions include ___________, ___________ and ___________.
2. If an athlete vomits, position the athlete on her or his ___________.
3. If an athlete faints and you do not suspect a head, neck or back injury, position the athlete on her or his ___________ and elevate the ___________ 8 to 12 inches.
4. For a known diabetic emergency, give the person ___________.
5. Possible clues of poisoning to look for when checking the scene include ___________, ___________, ___________ and ___________.
6. If poisoning is suspected, try to determine the ___________ and ___________ of poison taken and ___________ the poison was taken.
7. Heat- and cold-related emergencies (can/cannot) ___________ result in death.

STEPS OF FIRST AID FOR SUDDEN ILLNESS

Put the following first aid steps in the correct order for sudden illness. Write 1 in front of the first step to perform, 2 in front of the second step, etc.

____ Send someone to call 9-1-1 or local emergency number for life-threatening emergencies.

____ Check the scene for safety.
____ Help the athlete rest comfortably.
____ Check for life threatening conditions.
____ To minimize shock, keep the athlete from getting chilled or overheated.
____ Reassure the athlete.
____ Watch for changes in consciousness.

STEPS OF FIRST AID FOR POISONING

Put the following first aid steps in the correct order for poisoning. Write "1" in front of the first step to perform, "2" in front of the second step, etc.

____ Check the scene. Make sure it is safe to approach the athlete.
____ Check the athlete's consciousness, breathing and signs of circulation.
____ Care for life-threatening conditions.
____ Remove the athlete from the source of the poison, if necessary.
____ Call the Poison Control Center [(800) 222-1222] or 9-1-1 or the local emergency number.

STEPS OF FIRST AID FOR HEAT-RELATED EMERGENCIES

Put the following first aid steps in the correct order for heat-related emergencies. Write 1 in front of the first step to perform, 2 in front of the second step, etc.

____ Apply cold, wet cloths to the skin and fan the athlete.
____ If conscious, give the athlete small amounts of cool water to drink.
____ Get the athlete out of the heat.
____ Loosen tight clothing and remove perspiration-soaked clothing.
____ Send someone to call 9-1-1 or local emergency number if the athlete refuses water, vomits or starts to lose consciousness

STEPS OF FIRST AID FOR COLD-RELATED EMERGENCIES

Put the following first aid steps in the correct order for cold-related emergencies. Write 1 in front of the first step to perform, 2 in front of the second step, etc.

____ Send someone to call 9-1-1 or local emergency number.
____ Remove any wet clothing and dry the athlete.
____ Care for life-threatening conditions.
____ Move the athlete to a warm place, if possible.
____ Apply hot water bottles, chemical heat packs and other heat sources, if available.
____ Warm the athlete slowly by wrapping in blankets or putting on dry clothes.

SCENARIOS

Imagine yourself as the coach in the following situations. You have a first aid kit and your *Sports Safety Training Handbook*. Use your *Handbook* to answer the questions for this scenario, along with information you have learned in this course.

1. Toward the end soccer practice, one of your players complains of feeling ill and asks if he can go into the locker room to lie down. You don't see signals of any life-threatening conditions, but the athlete looks pale and acts slightly confused. (Put a "Y" [for yes] by actions you would take and an "N" [for no] by actions you should *not* take.)
   a. Your first action should be to—
      ____ Tell him to run laps to "run it off."
      ____ Immediately give him a large drink of a chilled sports beverage.
      ____ Have him sit down and rest and keep him from getting chilled or overheated.
      ____ Watch for changes in consciousness and breathing.
   b. As far as you know, the athlete has not suffered an injury. In addition, it is not particularly warm in the room, so you doubt heat is a factor. Your next action should be to—
      ____ Ask him if he wants to shower.
      ____ Ask him if he has diabetes or any other medical condition.
      ____ Ask him if he feels lightheaded, dizzy or nauseous.
      ____ Ask him if he has a headache or feels any other pain or pressure.
   c. If he is a diabetic, you should—
      ____ Ask him how long he has had diabetes.
      ____ Ask him what type of diabetes he has.
      ____ Give him glucose paste, glucose tablets, fruit juice, non-diet soft drink or candy to raise his sugar level.
   d. Send someone to call 9-1-1 or local emergency number if—
      ____ He has breathing difficulty or is breathing irregularly.
      ____ He complains of eating too much for lunch.
      ____ He has persistent chest pain or pressure or persistent pain in the abdomen.

____ He begins vomiting blood or passing blood.

____ He has seizures, sudden severe headache or sudden slurred speech or trouble speaking.

____ He is a diabetic and does not begin to feel better within 5 minutes after taking sugar.

e. If the athlete's condition does not worsen, you should—

____ Allow him to shower and leave.

____ Instruct him to seek medical attention if he does not begin to feel better.

____ Send him back into practice.

2. Toward the end of wrestling practice, an assistant coach comes in to your office to report that a number of wrestlers are complaining of headaches. The wrestling room "smells funny," he adds, asking if you'll check it out. You return with him to the wrestling room and as you enter you notice a mild, but persistent, chemical odor.
   a. Your immediate action should be to—(circle one)
      1. Send someone to call 9-1-1 or the local emergency number.
      2. Call the custodians to bring in fans.
      3. Have everyone go outside into fresh air.
      4. Call the fire department.
   b. Your next action should be to—(circle one)
      1. Check the conditions of the athletes and assistant coach.
      2. Find another room in which to continue the practice.
      3. Attempt to find the source of the chemical odor.
      4. All of the above.
   c. You recall that a newly refurbished mat had been installed in the room—which has no windows—over the weekend. What does this clue suggest? (circle one)
      1. The installation was not done correctly.
      2. There may be carpet glue fumes in the air.
      3. The practice was too strenuous for the conditions.
      4. You should check for rug burns.
   d. Believing that the athletes and coach are suffering from the inhalation of poisoning fumes, you take the following: (circle one)
      1. Call the Poison Control Center [(800) 222-1222] or 9-1-1or the local emergency number.
      2. Make sure the athletes and coach drink plenty of fluids.
      3. Send someone to call EMS personnel.
      4. All of the above.
3. On a sunny, warm summer day, your cycling team goes for a long, strenuous workout. When the team members return from the ride, they lay down on the ground under a large tree and begin to drink a sports beverage. As you join them to discuss strategies for an upcoming race, you notice that one cyclist is sitting on the ground near her bicycle, out in the sun. When you call over to her, you notice that she is quite flushed. Quickly you help her out of the sun, and in doing so you note that her skin is hot and dry. When you get her into the shade and offer liquid, she refuses it, complaining that her head hurts.
   a. Immediately you should ________________.
   b. Sensing that she is suffering from a heat-related emergency, you should do the following: (circle all that apply)
      1. Loosen tight clothing and remove perspiration-soaked clothing.
      2. Try to get her up to walk around.
      3. Have her lie on back with her feet raised 8–12 inches.
      4. Make her as comfortable as possible, regardless of how she sits.
      5. Fan her and apply wet cloths or cool/cold packs.
      6. Encourage her to drink water.

ANSWERS TO ACTIVITIES

MULTIPLE CHOICE

1. **a, b, d and e are correct** (Of the signals listed, only hunger is not typically a signal of serious illness.)
2. **a, b, c and d are correct** (All signals could indicate sudden illness.)
3. **a, b and e are correct** (Fainting, head injury or persistent chest pressure are all signals of potential serious illness; with vomiting, not feeling well, or poisonous plant exposure, calling 9-1-1 may not be necessary.)
4. **b, c, d and f are correct** (Always call 9-1-1 or the local emergency number if the athlete has not had a seizure before, for a long or repeated seizures, if the athlete is diabetic, or if the athlete does not immediately regain consciousness.)

5. **a, b, c and d are correct** (All fumes listed can be toxic.)
6. **a and c are correct** (Poisonous plants and many common chemicals can be absorbed through the skin.)
7. **a, b, c and d are correct** (All the listed factors can affect the risk of heat- and cold-related emergencies.)
8. **a, b and c are correct** (Sunburn is treated as a minor burn, not a heat-related illness; heat cramps, exhaustion and stroke are all forms of heat-related illness.)
9. **c and d are correct** (Frostbite and hypothermia are the only two types of cold-related emergencies.)
10. **b, c and d are correct** (Risk factors for hypothermia include poor circulation, age and use of diuretics, but not the unrelated condition glaucoma.)
11. **a, c, d and e are correct** (The signals of frostbite are white, yellow or blue skin; numbness; and waxy, cold skin.)
12. **a, c, d and e are correct** (All the listed things, except hyperactivity, are signals of hypothermia.)

MATCHING

1. c
2. f
3. g
4. e
5. d
6. h
7. a
8. b

TRUE/FALSE

1. T (Environmental extremes can contribute to heat- and cold-related emergencies.)
2. F (Care for the general illness, not a specific condition.)
3. F (If the athlete vomits, position the athlete on her or his side.
4. T (That the athlete has had a stroke may not be immediately apparent, but the signals of stroke are similar to those of other sudden illnesses.)
5. T (Food or drink can cause choking in an athlete who has fainted.)
6. T (Feeling ill persisting after the athlete takes sugar may indicate a diabetic emergency; the athlete needs medical attention.)
7. T (Substance abuse has become a major source of poisoning deaths.)
8. F (For any life-threatening condition [such as an unsafe scene, the child is unconscious, having trouble breathing or having seizures], call 9-1-1 or the local emergency number, or have someone else call if possible; otherwise contact the National Poison Control Center first for help.)
9. F (Save some of the vomit in case the hospital needs to analyze it to identify the poison.)
10. T (The normal red or pink coloring of the lips and some skin areas is caused by oxygenated blood, which becomes bluish when depleted of oxygen.)
11. T (Not everyone is allergic to insect bites and stings, but those who are can have a severe, life-threatening reaction.)
12. F (Wear disposable gloves. If a bee sting, remove the stinger by scraping away with a flat surface like a credit card. Otherwise, try to remove by grasping as close to skin as possible with tweezers).
13. F (The signals of Lyme disease—rash, fever, headache, weakness, joint and muscle pain—can begin a few days, a few weeks or longer after the bite occurred. In addition, not all signals may occur.)
14. T (Immobilizing the bitten area and keeping it *lower* than the heart help keep the poison from spreading throughout the body.)
15. T (Rabies is a life-threatening disease; immediately seek medical care after a bite from an animal suspected of having rabies.)
16. F (The three main factors affecting the body temperature are air temperature, humidity and wind.)
17. F (On the contrary, once the signals become apparent, the athlete's condition can quickly worsen.)
18. T (Cooling areas where there are large blood vessels helps cool the whole body most quickly.)
19. F (Hypothermia can occur when the body is exposed to any temperature significantly below body temperature.)
20. F (Rubbing causes further damage to soft tissues. Instead, *slowly* warm the affected part by soaking it in water no warmer than 105 degrees F.)

FILL-IN-THE-BLANKS

1. diabetes, epilepsy, and heart condition
2. side (this helps keep the airway open)
3. back, legs (this position helps the brain receive blood containing oxygen)
4. sugar (sugar is most likely what the diabetic's body needs; if not, it will not cause additional harm)
5. unusual odors, flames, smoke, open or spilled containers, open medicine cabinet, overturned or damaged plant

6. type, quantity or amount, when or time
7. can

STEPS OF FIRST AID FOR SUDDEN ILLNESS

The steps should be numbered in this order:

3 Send someone to call 9-1-1 or the local emergency number for life-threatening emergencies.
1 Check the scene for clues.
4 Help the athlete rest comfortably.
2 Check for life-threatening conditions.
5 To minimize shock, keep the athlete from getting chilled or overheated.
6 Reassure the athlete.
7 Watch for changes in consciousness.

STEPS OF FIRST AID FOR POISONING

1 **CHECK** the scene. Make sure it is safe to approach the athlete.
3 **CHECK** the athlete's consciousness, breathing and signs of circulation.
4 **CARE** for life-threatening conditions.
2 Remove the athlete from the source of the poison, if necessary.
5 Question the athlete, if conscious, and look for the source of the poison.
6 For any life-threatening condition (such as an unsafe scene, the child is unconscious, having trouble breathing or having seizures), **CALL** 9-1-1 or the local emergency number, or have someone else call if possible; otherwise contact the National Poison Control Center first for help.

STEPS OF FIRST AID FOR HEAT-RELATED EMERGENCIES

3 Apply cool, wet cloths to the skin and fan the athlete.
4 If conscious, give the athlete small amounts of cool water to drink.
1 Get the athlete out of the heat.
2 Loosen tight clothing and remove perspiration-soaked clothing.
5 Send someone to call 9-1-1 or the local emergency number if the athlete refuses water, vomits or starts to lose consciousness.

STEPS OF FIRST AID FOR COLD-RELATED EMERGENCIES

1 Send someone to call 9-1-1 or the local emergency number.
4 Remove any wet clothing and dry the athlete.
2 Care for life-threatening conditions.
3 Move the athlete to a warm place if possible.
6 Apply hot water bottles (as appropriate), chemical heat packs and other heat sources if available.
5 Warm the athlete *slowly* by wrapping in blankets or putting on dry clothes.

SCENARIOS

Scenario 1: Soccer player complaining of feeling ill

a. N, N, Y, Y (Do not *immediately* give the athlete anything to eat or drink without investigating his illness further. Never have an ill athlete "run it off.")
b. N, Y, Y, Y (Before allowing the athlete to go to the showers, investigate his illness further.)
c. N, N, Y (The duration or type of diabetes is not an important factor in determining the immediate care that you give.)
d. Y, N, Y, Y, Y, Y (All of these factors, *except* eating too much, could be serious.)
e. Y, Y, N (*Do not* return to play an athlete who feels ill.)

Scenario 2: Wrestling team with headaches

a. 3 (Since it seems likely there may be fumes in the room, the *first* step is to get everyone away from the danger.)
b. 1 (Once everyone is away from the danger, check those who may have been affected.)
c. 2 (Fumes are likely, but you do not need to diagnose the problem to provide care and avoid further risk to the athletes.)
d. 1 (Once you decide a poison may be involved, call the Poison Control Center or local emergency number as appropriate.)

Note: This injury may have been prevented—a careful check of the area before practice may have discovered the fumes problem.

Scenario 3: Bicyclist with heat-related emergency

a. Send someone to call 9-1-1 or the local emergency number. (This athlete has the signals of a late-stage heat emergency, heat stroke—refusing water is a serious sign—and needs medical attention as quickly as possible.)
b. 1, 4, 5, 6 (These are the appropriate actions for heat stroke—but not walking around or lying down with feet raised.)

Note: This emergency may have been prevented—this cyclist may have been more susceptible to a heat-related emergency because of a preexisting condition or because of not following safety guidelines such as maintaining adequate hydration.